Pacific Lady

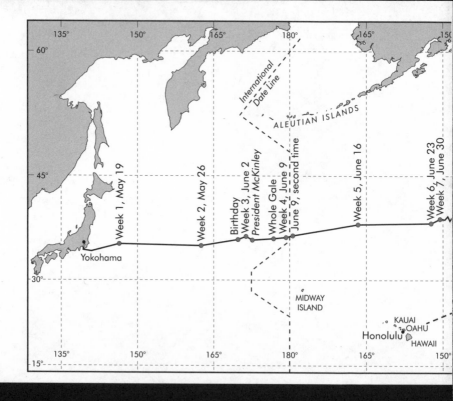

OUTDOOR LIVES

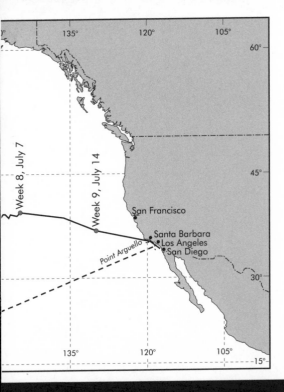

Pacific Lady

The First Woman to Sail Solo across
the World's Largest Ocean

Sharon Sites Adams *with* Karen J. Coates

Foreword by Randall Reeves

UNIVERSITY OF NEBRASKA PRESS | LINCOLN AND LONDON

Library of Congress Cataloging-in-Publication Data

Adams, Sharon Sites.
Pacific lady: the first woman to sail solo across the world's largest ocean / Sharon Sites Adams with Karen J. Coates; foreword by Randall Reeves.
    p. cm. — (Outdoor lives)
ISBN 978-0-8032-1138-4 (cloth: alk. paper)
1. Adams, Sharon Sites—Travel—Pacific Ocean.
2. Sailing, Single-handed—Pacific Ocean.
3. Sailors—United States—Biography.
4. Women sailors—United States—Biography.
    I. Coates, Karen J., 1971– II. Title. III. Series.

G530.A132A33 2008   910.9164902—dc22
[B] 2008010457

Set in Minion.
Designed by Ashley Muehlbauer.

For Ted, Chrisie, and Cyndy

My love

Contents

Illustrations

Following page 110

Diagrams

Foreword

RANDALL REEVES

I met Sharon by phone in the fall of 2003 at the end of a long, hot day of boat work. The sun had just set and I was washing up, musing over my aching back and the next day's tasks, when the phone rang. "Hello. This is Sharon Adams," said a perky and entirely unexpected voice. "My coauthor said you wished to speak with me."

I'm an avid boatman who has been dreaming or reading of blue-water cruising much of his life. In fact, this boat on which I'd worked for months, a thirty-one-foot Far East Mariner Ketch, was purchased precisely for that purpose. But I'd had no idea until the previous week of her historical links, that she was the same make, model, and vintage as *Sea Sharp II*, the boat Sharon sailed in her single-handed crossing of the Pacific.

This discovery was the result of a casual Internet search for anything unusual about my old boat. But after the initial find and its resulting elation, I began to realize that beyond mentions of Sharon and her accomplishments—she was the first woman to sail solo from California to Hawaii in 1965 and then, in 1969, the first woman to cross the entire Pacific Ocean alone from Yokohama to San Diego—no other information was available. No detailed history or voyage accounts of Sharon existed, and only one site discussed the potential of a biography in the works. Then just days after sending a note of introduction to Sharon's coauthor, here she was on the phone.

It is one thing to wish for a meeting and another thing altogether to get it. Standing in the middle of the boatyard and at the ragged end of a tiring day, I had no idea what to say, but Sharon didn't mind. We discussed my boat and her adventures. She asked with genuine interest what cruising I intended to do (extended, somewhere, someday) and assured me I'd got a good boat. She inquired about my self-steering device and, finding I had none, quickly offered to (and later did) send plans for the bulletproof, home-built wind vane she had used. She recommended the installation of a cabin-top bubble made of Plexiglas like the one she had on *Sea Sharp II* so that while on passage, I could safely see all around without going on deck. She praised the Mariner's easy handling and comfort below. "But what was she like in rough weather?" I asked. "Oh, just fine," came the confident voice on the phone, "I got knocked down once in fifty knots, but it was my own fault."

By the time of this conversation, Sharon's oceanic adventures were well in the past, but I found her stories to be fresh and relevant and told with a passion that suggested she had just come ashore. In setting her two records, she had single-handed well beyond eight thousand miles of open ocean, yet she was freely offering her advice to a man she'd never met and whose boat, at the time, didn't even float. We talked into the evening, and after a fatiguing day in the yard, the conversation did much to boost my flagging morale.

The remarkable nature of Sharon's achievements can be easy to miss these days. For one thing, the age of air travel has shrunk the world to such a degree that the idea of crossing an ocean now seems unspectacular—it can be accomplished in a day's flight. So, a few facts to set the stage. First, sailing a small boat is slow work in any weather. *Sea Sharp II*'s top speed was around six knots, but due to the vagaries of wind, her average speed for the seventy-four days it took to cross the Pacific was just four knots, or about as fast as a fit person can jog. And a relaxing vacation it was not! Sharon was solely responsible for the care of her little craft—shortening sail in foul weather, piling it on in fair, and repairing whatever might break—twenty-four hours a day, day after day.

Second, Sharon chose to cross what is by far the world's largest ocean. At a staggering sixty-four million square miles, the Pacific is twice the size of the Atlantic, covers a full third of the planet, and is so vast that the area of the United States, including Alaska and Hawaii, could fit into it sixteen times with room to spare. Sharon's route between Yokohama and San Diego traces a rhumb line course of almost six thousand miles, or the equivalent of heading east out of Los Angeles and traveling as far as Casablanca in West Africa, eight time zones away. And unlike the tropical island–paradise typically depicted in television and movies, this part of the Pacific is entirely open, uninterrupted, and often stormy water.

Another differentiating factor is technology. While crossing an ocean may never be easy, the abundance of electronic devices now available have taken much of the difficulty and some of the risk out of making the passage. Global positioning systems, radar, satellite telephones, and laptop computers that receive graphical weather reports and send e-mail over ham radio signals are considered standard equipment by many small-boat captains today. And with them, the contemporary voyager can know his position to within a few feet by the push of a button; he can quickly know the state of the weather anywhere in the world, and can stay in daily contact with those ashore.

In contrast, Sharon found her position on the ocean the old-fashioned way. She used a sextant (technology already in use in the 1700s) to measure the sun's angles and then reduced those angles to coordinates by doing famously difficult math. At best, on any given day, Sharon knew her position to within a mile or so. She only knew what weather was approaching by looking at the sky. And though she did have a radio for the Yokohama to San Diego run, it failed to operate. For much of her two and a half months at sea, Sharon was utterly isolated from the rest of the world, beyond reach or rescue, and entirely dependent on her own skills and the soundness of her boat.

Put simply, ocean crossing is a most committing endeavor; and when Sharon did it, there were those who weren't sure a woman could or should. This highlights another remarkable aspect of Sharon's accomplishments—she was one of the first *female* single-handers.

That women participate alongside men in many sports, including sailing, is now largely taken for granted. For example, the fact that the second-place finisher in the 2000–2001 Vendee Globe—a grueling, solo, nonstop, around-the-world sailing race—was a twenty-four-year-old Englishwoman named Ellen MacArthur is unlikely to spark anything but admiration among her contemporaries. But such was not the case in 1965 when Sharon was roundly snubbed by the local yacht club just after becoming the first woman to sail from California to Hawaii in a twenty-five-foot Folkboat. And days after her arrival in Honolulu, she was accosted on the docks by a local yachtsman who berated her for such an unwomanly exploit as crossing an ocean.

By the time Sharon began her career as a voyager, the world's oceans had been single-handed many times by men. The first authenticated solo crossing of the Pacific occurred in 1882 and is credited to Bernard Gilboy, who made it from San Francisco to Australia (almost) in his small, double-ended yacht, the *Pacific*. Six years earlier the first west-to-east solo crossing of the Atlantic was completed by a fisherman named Alfred Johnson in an open, twenty-foot dory. These were the first two of many early single-handed passages that include now-forgotten but then-famous names like R. T. McMullen, John MacGregor, Albert Andrews, and Howard Blackburn. The crowning achievement in early cruising came in 1898 when Joshua Slocum proved what had been widely held impossible—he circumnavigated the globe in a small boat named *Spray*.

Women have entered this scene only lately. For example, Sharon's unprecedented 1969 crossing of the Pacific in *Sea Sharp II* came a full eighty-seven years after Gilboy's. In 1952 Ann Davidson, in her twenty-three-foot *Felicity Ann*, was the first woman to cross the Atlantic, seventy-six years after Alfred Johnson's passage, and she wasn't seconded until 1969 by Ingeborg von Heister. Seventy-eight years after Slocum crossed his own wake, Krystyna Chojnowska-Liskiewicz became the first woman to circumnavigate the globe. Like many of their male counterparts, these women and their accomplishments have been reduced simply to names on lists of early sailing records.

Some months after our first phone call, Sharon and I met in person at a Mariner Owners Association gathering in Los Angeles. The event organizers, Bill Kranidis and Tony West, Mariner owners and passionate advocates for the preservation of these now-vintage yachts, were excited to have Sharon attend and deliver a lecture she'd been sharing for years with other interested groups. I had the honor of having invited Sharon, who immediately agreed, showing her enthusiasm and the single-hander's knack by making the long trip down from her Oregon home by car and by herself.

Sharon stood next to her small display table, spry and alert, wearing a hot-pink blouse and clearly enjoying the attention of other sailboat owners. During earlier correspondence, I had learned that pink was Sharon's trademark color. To the consternation of many in 1969, she had asked that the decks of *Sea Sharp II* be painted pastel pink, that a pink stripe be added to the hull, and that hot pink be integrated into some of the sails. And on the voyage, Sharon sewed a hot-pink dress that she intended to wear on arrival day.

At the end of her talk and slide show, one of the sailors in the audience asked, "Why did you want to cross an entire ocean alone?" Her answer: "I didn't see what there was about it that I couldn't do."

These few sentences can only hint at the complexities involved in being a woman adventurer of forty-odd years ago, and it is a mark of Sharon's essential courage that while undertaking physical and social challenges never before attempted by someone of her gender, she did not abandon her own view of womanhood. Women in sports today owe a debt of gratitude to the likes of Sharon Adams. I invite you to enjoy this book, so long in coming, about a solo sailing pioneer.

Preface

KAREN J. COATES

In October 1964 Sharon Sites learned to sail. On June 12, less than eight months later, the thirty-five-year-old widow set out from California on a twenty-five-foot Danish Folkboat named *Sea Sharp* headed for Honolulu. Thirty-nine days after that she made world history, docking in Waikiki, becoming the first woman to single-hand from the mainland United States to Hawaii. Sharon gained instant fame; she was praised for bravery and chastised for foolishness. What right had she to sail the seas? What hope she gave to all women! The public's views diverged.

But Sharon wasn't done.

On May 12, 1969, she cast off from a wharf in Yokohama, Japan, in a Mariner 31 named *Sea Sharp II*, beginning a six-thousand-mile journey to San Diego. Alone again. Seventy-five days later she succeeded, becoming the first woman to single-hand the Pacific.

In all, Sharon set five world records: first woman to single-hand the waters between the U.S. mainland and Hawaii, first woman to single-hand the Pacific, first woman to set two such records, longest distance sailed by a woman, and most days a woman had ever spent at sea alone. Sharon did all that in an era without GPS, cell phones, e-mail, or Internet. She sailed in what was still a technological dark age for sailors. Sharon Sites Adams is no feminist. She did not sail the Pacific to prove anything about women. Sharon Sites Adams sailed the seas because she could.

Acknowledgments

Ruth, you are my best friend. Debbie, Randall, Jason, Millie, Tom, and Jan: Your help, faith, and encouragement got me through this endeavor. "Thanks" is inadequate. You each know what you mean to me. In addition, a special salute to every proud Mariner owner. Fair winds and happy sailing.

Pacific Lady

Alone

There is no loneliness wider than the single-handed sailor's. She is cast for days, for months, beneath an endless breadth of sky atop a plain of eternal blue. So blue. As far as the eye can see—blue. Tinted gray or green, light or dark, but forever blue.

Her life becomes confined to a small plot, just a couple dozen feet long and a fraction thereof wide. Her mind dances with insanity, depression, hallucination, self-defeat. Some of these or all of these—life alone on water drags the sailor down. Whether she plunges beneath the surface or whether she returns to the world on land are questions that color every day at sea. Every single day.

I was not prepared for that, in either of my record-setting voyages. Experience does not deaden the sting of loneliness at sea.

I had hardly sailed before embarking on my first journey from California to Hawaii in the spring of 1965. I didn't know how scared I should have been. I was too naive to know that loneliness would be my greatest fear, my nemesis, the gremlin that would get me. And so it was again four years later, when I set sail for the second time, departing from Japan for San Diego.

Today it's different. Sailors have winds of another kind. Technology leads them through the doldrums and keeps their spirits intact; it connects them to the world in ways that old-time sailors never were. Technology has the power to eradicate aloneness. Today's solitary sailors have satellite phones, global positioning systems, e-mail and Internet, solar panels and ICOM equipment; so many gadgets to keep their bearings on the ocean, in the world, and with themselves. I'm just now learning to use the Internet. But sailors today, they know where they are and the world knows where they are. Forty years ago we single-handers sailed unknown. We navigated with the sun. We had to believe that mathematical formulas would get us to our destination, though we never knew for sure until land appeared. Our friends didn't know, couldn't know, when we would return or whether we would survive, and we—I—on the boat didn't know. Neither could I share the events of my day.

I had a World War II air force sextant. I had kerosene running lights and inside the boat a gimbaled light, two compasses, and a Timex watch that could be set to the second. With my Zenith transoceanic shortwave radio, I could check the atomic clock at the National Institute of Standards and Technology in Boulder, Colorado, for the official government time. I could listen to the radio as I bobbed along, but I could not talk back. I heard baseball games and news of the world, but no one heard from me.

Sometimes I heard gossip about me, though. It came one morning on the *Breakfast Club*, a broadcast from Chicago hosted by Don McNeil. I can almost hear that voice now: "Have you all heard about the young housewife who is sailing alone in her boat to Hawaii?" McNeil told his audience it would be a dangerous, dubious idea for a strong man. "But for a woman without experience, can you imagine?"

I remember the chuckle, coming from his sidekick.

"What's so funny?" McNeil asked him.

"I was thinking about buying my wife a boat like hers."

I'll betcha they never guessed I could hear them, way out there in my housewife's boat. I heard them, loud and clear, but they couldn't hear me. No one could.

And yet I chose that solitude. I chose to endure it twice on the world's largest ocean. I wanted to cross those waters so badly—why? Just to say I had? Truth be told, I'm not entirely sure, even after all these years. I just felt the need to do it once I'd dreamed up the idea.

I am not the greatest sailor, I admit that. And loneliness is not everyone's adversary, as it is mine. Yet not every sailor could do it, could stand being alone so long. Some sailors simply couldn't endure their own minds. What does it take? I have no idea whether it's simple determination or something much more. But if I am determined to do something, God willing, I will. I only ask myself whether I am able. If I am, I'll do it.

I have always been that way. I remember myself at five or six years old, how determined I was. I grew up in the outdoors of rural Oregon. The neighborhood boys cut the limbs off the trees to keep me out of their tree house, but I defied them. I shimmied up a rope as they did. I wanted to be up there, and why not? I could do anything the boys could. That was my attitude all through school. I was the first woman in my high school who didn't take home economics; why should I? I had been doing the family cooking since I was twelve, so I took mechanical drawing instead.

Critics have accused me of being too independent, and I'm sure that's true. Reporters lambasted me when I sailed to Hawaii. One asked, "Why?" when it would have been cheaper to fly. They called me a foolish housewife. They psychoanalyzed me. Some asked who gave me the right to sail the ocean alone. But I didn't need permission; that much I knew. Others even said I hadn't really done it, I hadn't really sailed. What? Did they think I'd camped on an island all those nights? Or hopped on a cruise ship? Or flew across the ocean incognito, then rustled up a little harbor boat to create the illusion of my arrival?

Yes, my headstrong nature has cost me a few friendships. But it's also defined my life.

And I've thought about those things, out there alone on the Pacific. Not much else fills the mind when the wind doesn't blow, when the sails luff. Life becomes a purgatory in still waters.

At other times, life is a tempest, riled and mighty. I endured several gale-force winds that rolled the ocean and hurled me against the cockpit coaming, bruising my rib cage. My body turned blue, blue like the sea. Every breath drew pain. Pain and discomfort are more fearsome when faced alone.

It was so damp, too. Always damp. A damp so thick it penetrated my clothing and gnawed at my skin. So damp I could not sharpen pencils and my paper grew too soft for me to write. I packed my clothes inside a sleeping bag, hoping body heat would dry them. But the air hung so thick that I could almost wring it out.

And the gray. Oh, the gray, at times lasting a week or more, it painted my mood. A dreadful gray. Should I scream? Or cry? Or run outside my little hatch and keep on running? I thought about it. I could not get warm some days. I tried to surround myself in vibrant colors, in self-made cheer that would outdo the sky and sea. You know, I love the color pink, hot pink, anything painted in that electrifying hue. So I could not bear a life of gray, nor of fog. Sometimes the fog swirled around me, wrapping me deep inside its blanket. It seemed to come on cat paws, just as Carl Sandburg had written.

I devised little ways of enduring; every sailor has her own. At times, I talked to myself, babbling to my tape recorder and writing in my diary. It's true, I survived through communication—even though I was speaker and audience all the same. I talked to that recorder like a pal. I called it "you" and bestowed it with the quality of human companionship. Now those conversations remain as record; they're testimony to my travels. When I look back on those entries, I learn things about myself and I am transported back to my days at sea.

Any single-hander will suffer mercurial moods. Lows so low, the heart plummets to ocean's bottom, anchored in darkness and cold. And highs so high, they stretch wide wings of hope over our little journeys on water. I can hear those highs in my recorder: "Top o' the mornin' to you all! I've had a wonderful night's sleep. The wind is from the northwest at eighteen miles per hour. There's not a cloud in the sky. Perfect!"

But moods shifted as quickly as the breeze; and at another time with no wind and a wicked headache, I was a different Sharon: "I have kicked, screamed, beat with my fists, slammed pans together and—oh, I just can't tell you. This is the kind of frustration that could drive me overboard. I could take a hammer and swing and swing—strike out at everything, beat this boat to death."

There were days of stagnant grayness, weighting my veins with lifeless blood. My pulse stirred with each flicker of wind, but for so long I huddled beneath a wall of fog. This happens to every sailor, I'm sure, and it happened to me more than once:

A few more swells and an occasional ripple across the water from the southeast. I trimmed sails. Twenty minutes later the ripples approached from the north. I trimmed again. After expending all that energy, I looked up at the bits of nylon yarn tied to the shrouds to show wind direction. They were lifting slightly—and pointing directly at each other! My hopes of moving again were shattered. Now we are sitting as before. There is not a breath of air. "Thy will be done." But the Lord and I are not in agreement at the moment.

My fate idled on still water beneath still sky that day. A few al-tocumulus clouds drifted slowly overhead, a whisper of wind way up there, but nothing for me and the boat. I did what I always did when stuck in such a rut: I busied myself with housekeeping. I repaired all things broken, greased and oiled all parts I could reach, scrubbed salt from the deck, polished the chrome. There was nothing more I could do for the boat; there was little more I could do for me.

Always, the worst was not knowing. Will the stagnant air continue two hours? Two days? Two weeks? No sailor knows when she's in the middle of the sea. At least a storm gives winds to whip, rain to beat, something alive to fight. The calm lends nothing. Like shadowboxing, the heft of my punch would disappear in static air.

This is why loneliness festers in the doldrums. The battle is in the mind, and the mind is never beaten. You read a book, and it exhausts you. You write a letter; eventually it ends. You sew, and one day the dress is done. I once made a dress, a pink sundress, and there in the doldrums I had nearly finished it. It made me sad. I had one more arm facing, a hem, and a ruffle, and then it would be ready. But for what? No one else was there to see it, to see me in that dress. I almost ripped it apart just to start again, to give me something to do.

One day I simply told my recorder, "It hasn't been a very good day." On that day, I had sailed just five miles, but I had eaten more than that in food. When you're out on the water for weeks on end, you must count your food in days. I figured I was stocked for ninety. When we traveled swiftly—I mean the boat and I—I had no problem with what I ate. Oh, but the mind wrestles with the stomach when the boat slows. If I didn't move, didn't log the miles for a particular day, I didn't deserve to eat. That's what my brain would decide. I always checked my log to see when and what I had eaten last.

Once, I drifted two miles backward—far, far worse than standing still. To a sailor, each mile backward doubles the distance of failure. Twelve miles back really means twenty-four behind the goal of moving ahead. How could I eat? My mind played good cop and bad cop, one half thinking I deserved no food, the other knowing I needed sustenance. Still, in my heart I knew the truth: I wouldn't get anywhere without food.

So much thought of eating made me hungry all the time. I had no more cookies, no more candy, and I kept lusting for a cheese sandwich. Couldn't someone please bring me a cheese sandwich? A glass of cold milk? I desperately craved the things I couldn't have.

Life at sea was forever a psychological game, with the enormity of the ocean holding dominion over my mind. The Pacific is so vast that it can't fit onto one chart alone. Just east of the dateline, in midocean, the time comes when a sailor changes charts. Before that time, I always felt I was sailing uphill to no particular destination. My first chart ended in the middle of the ocean and dropped off to nowhere. I knew how Columbus's crew felt when they thought he might sail off the edge of the earth. Can you imagine? When I changed charts, I could see home, I could see land, I could see it in my head, I could see it printed on paper.

And still, there was so much more to do, so much farther to go under such leaden skies. One day the sun would shine again—it would have to. I knew that. I lit the oven and dried my socks and gloves and waited for a change in weather. I hung pants, shirts, foul-weather gear. I hung my sleeping bag one section at a time from the open oven door. And I tried to soothe my soul any way I could.

Sometimes the sea converses with lonely sailors. It talks. Really. Single-handers know this well. The ocean's rolls and swells become the voices of imagined companions. Some sailors begin to see the people in their heads. Hallucinations guide them through solitude or push them over the bow. "They shouted and whispered, laughed and giggled, tittered, coughed, and mumbled," Hannes Lindemann describes his ocean-borne friends, in *Alone at Sea*. "Their voices became so clear that I finally joined in the discussions."

Joshua Slocum was one of the greatest sailors to have lived. His story, *Sailing Alone Around the World*, published in 1900, remains something of a legend in sailing circles. It's one of America's best adventure books. Slocum survived a nasty storm with help from a friend. That fellow sailor advised him on foul weather and seafaring wisdom. He promised to return whenever needed. He was, he told Slocum, the pilot of the *Pinta*, reborn from his fifteenth-century voyage with Christopher Columbus. Then the storm broke, and the man disappeared. Slocum never saw him again.

But you know, we sailors have this: Even in the worst of times, we see the best of nature's beauty. On calm seas, the water acted like mirrors beneath my boat, reflecting the details of gooney birds floating beside me. I heard, in the center of an ocean, an utter silence broken only by the faint sound of a sail crinkling in the air. I drifted with sleek sharks that circled me and scratched their backs on the bottom of the boat. I watched the boat's wake spread like a silver lace fan behind me. Many times I witnessed the disappearance of horizon as sky melded with water to form a belly that ate me whole. And I drifted in that misty tomb, wet and tired and often too annoyed to appreciate the magnificence of it all.

Other times, I relished the wonder of the universe. On perfectly clear nights, the ocean reflected the heavens and the horizon blurred. It was as though our world lay in God's hands like a snow globe. When God shook, the boat and I floated in a mesmerizing swirl of stars.

I used to wait and plan and prepare and wait some more for a full moon. A full moon on a clear night struck the horizon like a blazing ball. It cast dancing moonbeams upon the sea, like a luminous wedge of pie. Always the moon crusted the edge of pie, and always we sat at its pinpoint. As it rose above, the moon kept its spotlight upon us, never veering, never leaving, forever thrusting us in the center of that heavenly world. And then as it dipped to sea again, the moon resumed its perch on the edge of the pie, still casting its farthest rays to us. We were but one lonely little speck on nature's majestic face.

I've seen a green flash, too, that extraordinary optical phenomenon. It's a refraction of light that depends on atmospheric conditions, the temperature, and the point from which a person views the spectacle. At sea level, a sailor might see just a second of green shaped in an oval on the horizon. You have to be looking. You have to be waiting, and I waited a lot. When you finally see one, it's beyond description. I don't have the ability or the words to convey the beauty of what I saw.

And many times it seemed the sun set herself just for me, all in pink. I was drenched in pink! The sky was pink and the water reflected the pink and the world was pink, all around me, pink. On land you have mountains and trees that slice into the color of a setting sun. But on water nothing obstructs the prism. It envelops the sailor. I became pink like the sunset.

God has blessed me with these things. God has shown me glimpses of a fantastic world. There's something so much greater than me, than we; I know that now. It is so lovely, so calming, so peaceful and serene. And I have no adequate words for it. We do not have language fitting for the world I've seen. I can dredge up memories; I can relay my thoughts within the confines of language. But nothing truly describes. Nothing suffices. Even the greatest words become a small boat on a vast sea of experience.

And that, I think, may be the single-handed sailor's greatest curse, for the majesty must be digested alone. Alone with the boat, the sea, and Mother Nature. And forever alone with the mind and its memories.

PART ONE

Out to Sea

ONE

A Widow Finds the Sea

I took him home and nursed him. I rented a hospital bed and put him in our living room. I gave him formula and painkillers, watching his spirit wither. He was fed through a tube and lost a hundred pounds. We lived in a cramped little one-bedroom duplex in West L.A., just behind the dental office where I worked. In that small neighborhood, my world unfolded—job and home, life, and eventually death. The death of my husband.

Chuck had cancer. Fate sent me the sweetest, motherly licensed vocational nurse to care for him through the day, though I went back and forth every hour or so between house and office just to hold his hand for a few minutes or to say a few words. Before the end, he couldn't talk. I would talk to him, but he couldn't even smile. He could do little more than move a finger if he wanted my help. Ten weeks this went on. Then he slid into his final coma. Like that, I watched my husband die.

It had started with general discomfort—Chuck said he just didn't feel good. He hurt when he ate, and he would push on his chest to get the food down. I persuaded him to see a doctor, and the doctor told him it was cancer of the stomach. They operated in early spring, but they didn't take anything out. They just sewed him back up, "too far gone," nothing they could fix. Cancer had eaten everything from his large intestine to his esophagus. He couldn't even swallow. They told me he didn't have long, and they were right. It went so fast. Chuck died quickly.

After it happened, I took Chuck's ashes to Bolin Lake in southern Oregon, as he had wished, where we had camped and hiked and breathed the fresh mountain air. I drove a rough forest service road to the spot we had "discovered," a place of happy memories. It would remain pristine. I buried him there on a hillside beneath tall trees, high above a lake, leaving my husband in peace by a circle of deep blue water.

Chuck died in May two weeks before his forty-second birthday. When he was gone, I returned to the routines I knew, to the full-time job I'd had for twelve years. Fillings, extractions, crowns, and bridges—they occupied my days and paid my rent. But I was lonely. Widowed at thirty-four, I was much too young to start marking time. I was looking for something else, but I had no idea what. Then one day, in that serendipitous way that happens in movies (and that sometimes happens in real life), I went for a drive that changed my life. I was returning home from church on a crisp October Sunday. The sun shone brightly. I could have turned left, but instead I kept going straight toward the new Marina del Rey. I had heard about it at work; everyone had. It was going to be the biggest man-made marina in the world, emerging in our midst in Los Angeles. Ironically, I lived and worked about a mile from the ocean and never went near it. I had grown up in Central Oregon with its high desert country of sagebrush and juniper, cattle ranches and lumber mills, bucolic fields dissected by burbling streams. I knew great forests in the West, I knew the arid landscape of the

Southwest, and the freeways and skyscrapers and overhead jets of Los Angeles. But the ocean I had never known.

So I drove toward the tall masts, toward boats tugging at their mooring lines. Marina del Rey eventually grew to encompass restaurants, shops, high-rise apartments, and whole families living aboard their boats on the water—an entire community unified in salt water and sail. The world would come together there, against the sea. But in 1964 it was just the beginning, just a few skeleton buildings, just a few boats and so many empty docks spreading like concrete fingers into the water.

I sat and watched the boats zigzagging their way up the channel. Now I know they were tacking—that's what it's called. But that day, I wondered how those sailors knew what to do. How did the boats know where to go? I was intrigued.

And that was it, my transformation. My genesis. It was honestly that much chance, or karma or kismet, that brought me to the ocean. I looked up and saw a billboard for the Al Adams Sailing School, and I thought, "Why not?"

I copied the number, slipped it into my purse, and dug it out a few weeks later. The woman on the other end of the line told me I fit all the requirements for enrolling, despite the landlocked nature of my life. I had $50, a notebook, and pencil. Nothing more was needed. Nothing more than the will to learn. Class met on Monday evenings, four times for group lecture, followed by four one-hour private lessons on a twenty-one-foot day sailer. And with that, I would learn to sail. I showed up, and my life changed.

Al Adams was an obvious man of the sea, surrounded by all manner of memorabilia that spoke of sailing. He had model ships, seashells, and sailing pennants, plaques, and trophies. He began our lessons with nomenclature. We learned the terminology, a new language, so that when we climbed aboard the boat, we would know the difference between a sheet and a halyard. We would know the meanings of port, starboard, bow, stern, winch, cleat, jib, genny, and main. When we were instructed to do something, we would be able to handle it. I learned a whole new vocabulary. All the parts of a boat and all the parts and properties of a sail—peak, tack, clew, foot, roach, leech, luff, panels, miter. I learned to tie basic knots—bowline, clove hitch, figure eight. I lay awake at night, my mind awhirl with words.

On October 23, 1964, the indoctrination came to fruition with my first private sail. I arrived for class an hour early, with butterflies looping through my stomach. The boat in question was a twenty-one-foot fiberglass sloop named *Howdy*, which had a mainsail, small genny, and keel. I climbed aboard with Al, who demonstrated how to sit at the helm and how to move from one side to the other. We cast off the last line beneath a ten-knot breeze, gliding smoothly out of the slip.

I learned that *Howdy* and I were part of nature, that we must be in order to go. Sailing is an intimate venture, and I learned to feel the breeze against my cheek, the rocking boat beneath my feet. A sailor must intuit the air, its speed and changes in direction. She must trim her boat for the fickle water and breeze. Her actions must grow instinctive, or she will not move efficiently nor do her boat justice. She must become an arbiter of the elements.

We practiced tacking, jibing, reaching, and running. We sailed in and out of an empty slip. I was free, gliding inside the harbor, the boat responding to my maneuvers. When I euphorically slid *Howdy* back into her place, Al got up and left me alone on the boat. He pushed me out of the slip and with a grin on his face said, "Now you take her back out and repeat what we just did—and bring her back to me."

"You wouldn't dare, you wouldn't dare!" I screamed back at him.

But he did. And I did it, too. Less than an hour after setting foot to deck for the first time in my life, I had sailed alone. I left alone and I returned alone, and I had fallen in love with this new world.

I was in love with the boat. It was a passion that swept me off the land and rocked me gently on its waves. After one lesson, I *knew* I was meant for the sea. Three weeks later I walked into Al's office to order my first boat. I didn't know much, but I knew what I wanted to do. I wanted to sail outside the harbor, maybe as far as Catalina, twenty-two miles off the coast. The boat had to be fit for the task. It had to be small enough for me to sail solo but big enough for me to fix a meal and sleep aboard.

I ordered a twenty-one-foot fiberglass sloop with keel, which had room enough to sit in the cabin. It came equipped with two sleeping bunks, a two-burner portable stove, and a head. I chose a champagne-colored hull and cabin sides, white decks, white trim, and turquoise cushions and interior. It cost me about $3,000, and I waited impatiently, bubbling inside for the next two weeks until her delivery put her in my possession.

She was christened the day before Thanksgiving 1964, on a brisk and windy morning. I started working at dawn, splicing dock lines and readying my new treasure. I thought nothing of turkey and stuffing, but all about champagne smacking that bow and the fact that she was mine. I named her after my car, a Chevrolet Impala Super Sport. That car was a silver beauty with chrome and silver Naugahyde. I paid $3,800 in cash for it new, and it had everything—air conditioning, radio, all the luxuries of the day. It was so pretty; it even sported my initials, SS, on the back. I decided to copy the name and call my new boat *Super Sport*.

That Thanksgiving, I declined dinner invitations with friends and spent the holiday with *Super Sport* instead. We practiced tacking and jibing inside the harbor, sticking close to shore and getting to know each other's grooves. We didn't go very far before I brought her back to the slip, but she slid right in, never touching the dock. I was tickled with my own aptitude.

From then on we were inseparable, the two of us, exploring all the nuances of Marina del Rey. I slept on her and ate on her, spending more time on the boat than I did at home. *Super Sport* became my life. I waxed and polished, scrubbed and beautified, until one day about two weeks later. I was eating lunch in the cockpit and addressing Christmas cards when I suddenly picked up my pen in midaddress and said to myself, "I bet I could sail to Hawaii." Simple as that, the thought was there. I don't know why, except that Hawaii is the only thing out there beyond Catalina and I suddenly had a notion to try it.

Al was walking along the dock with a new student. I put down my cards and stepped in front of him.

"I'm gonna sail to Hawaii."

He looked at me. "That's nice," and he walked on.

The idea plagued me, day and night, for two weeks. I couldn't wipe it way, couldn't sleep, couldn't think of anything else. Men had done it; I had read about them. I didn't know that no woman had, and that had nothing to do with my fixation anyway. I simply didn't know what about the idea was unattainable or why I couldn't succeed. (Of course, I hadn't yet been outside the breakwater, but never mind that.) Finally, I called Al's secretary and made an appointment to see him.

"I'm serious; I'm gonna sail to Hawaii," I blurted out across his office desk.

"With whom?" he asked.

"*Super Sport.*"

"Oh, no you're not."

"Oh, yes I am."

"I'm not sure you could get that boat to Catalina. It's not gonna go to Hawaii."

There was silence, a long silence, followed by a chuckle. "You can't mean it," Al said with a smirk.

I left that office more determined than ever.

Shortly after the holidays, a fleet of similar sloops formed a sailing association, and I was voted secretary-treasurer. We organized our first event, a full-day regatta. The rules required at least one teammate, so I asked a fellow student, another woman. We were the only females to enter.

On race day we took to the water early, practicing our starts and feeling the wind. When the gun fired, we were first to cross the line, upwind of the fleet. We held that position all the way through the course, fending off several challengers. We won. I was so excited, I sailed *Super Sport* back to her slip, leapt to the dock, and forgot to tie her up.

My companion and I ate lunch with our competitors, then we hit the water again. The second race didn't fare as well—I made a bad approach for the starting line, which cost us precious time. We had to jibe and form a new approach, which put us fourth in line. We never made up for that mistake, and we finished in second place.

That tied us for first overall, so the race committee held a conference and decided to hold a race between the two tied boats. The winds had built, blowing twenty miles per hour. We were exhausted, but this was our only chance. When we hit the starting line the third time, new breath filled our sails and spirits. Both teams raced evenly the entire first leg, but then we slowly pulled ahead. One inch, two inches, three. On the final leg, we pulled away. Our lee rail hit the water, soaking us with spray, but we didn't care. We crossed that finish line and took home the first-place trophy.

I knew my life had taken a new tack. I was going to Hawaii. Alone.

TWO

Fit for the Journey

Of course, I hadn't thought anything through, hadn't thought of all the particulars or the possibilities. I knew nothing of navigation; how would I find the islands? I was petite, with the muscles of an office clerk; how could I hoist the sails in heavy weather? How would I fix the boat when something broke? What if I got sick? Or hurt? Or caught in a storm or stranded or shoved off course or tossed overboard and eaten by sharks?

Al showed me films, footage of the open sea, with every intention of discouraging me. I still wanted to go. He showed me damage wrought by big waves and railing storms; I was not deterred. He asked me to imagine myself out there, alone against ocean and sky. I could think of no challenge more rousing.

Finally, Al sighed and said he would help me find a suitable craft that could carry me safely across 2,500 miles of unbroken, unpredictable sea.

It was early in the year of 1965 when the search began. From then on, little else mattered to me. I had saved some money through the years, but not a lot. I would work with what I had. I spent every hour off, every spare moment, scouring the coast up and down, searching marinas for a seaworthy vessel. I read the want ads, looking for a boat as though panning for gold. Then one day it surfaced in the Redondo Beach harbor.

I discovered her under full cover, a ten-year-old, twenty-five-foot Danish Folkboat—a spacious, wooden sea lover. As they peeled her cover back, I stood in awe. I could see my reflection in her sides, varnished to such a sheen. I said nothing, being so stunned by her beauty. I just touched and looked and dreamed. At thirty-four, I'd found a new love.

Folkboats are family boats designed to brave the turbulent northern European waters. They have been called clinkers, with hulls of overlapping wooden planks. This Folkboat, and others like it, had a good reputation on open waters. But the Folkboat does not have stanchions and lifelines and stern pulpits, nor is it self-bailing. In other words it's a very seaworthy boat, but it is not equipped for single-handing. It would require considerable time and serious expense to make her fit my needs. It would cost $10,000 (more than $50,000 in today's prices) for the boat, the rigging, and all the necessary alterations. It would take almost every dollar I had.

Was I crazy? I could buy roundtrip airfare for a smidgen of that cost, and I'd get to Hawaii in five hours with little effort. But it wasn't Hawaii itself; it was getting there that became my dream. The journey itself was what I needed in my heart, in my bones.

I took the Folkboat out for a trial. I held her tiller and I felt a connection. We fit, like old family friends. When I returned her to the boatyard, she was hauled out of the water and inspected, inch by inch, plank by plank, for two days. Nothing was wrong. I plunked down my money, and on March 6, 1965, she became mine.

"We have two immediate jobs," Al told me. The first was properly rigging the boat; the second, getting me into a physically fit condition capable of handling the task ahead.

I quit my job. After twelve years in the same office, I pranced into work and told Dr. Wolf I wouldn't be returning. I gave him eight weeks notice, and then I'd be off to sea. He thought I was joking until I informed him of the boat and all my plans. Most people thought I was joking at first, until they saw the commitment in my eyes. The disbelievers, the people who didn't know me, they called me names—crazy, kooky, stupid, psychotic. I was all these things in the public eye.

Never mind what they thought. I had work that needed to be done. My boat needed bigger winches to give her more power. We had to raise her cockpit seven inches, to make her self-bailing. This was accomplished by installing through-hull fittings, sea valves, and scupper pipes, and by building the cockpit's sole above the waterline so that water shipped in would not empty into the bilge, but would instead drain without being pumped. Two hand-operated bilge pumps were placed beneath the cockpit at such an angle that I could work them while sitting at the helm. The rudder was reinforced with Monel fastenings, and a stronger tiller was made. Bronze cheek plates were installed on the rudder and tiller for added strength. Stanchions, lifelines, and pulpits were specially designed. The stern pulpit, larger than found on many boats, served as the framework for a canvas dodger that wrapped around the aft two-thirds of the cockpit; that would afford me some protection from many days of winds and water.

The boat had to be equipped for steering herself at times so I could navigate, trim sails, cook meals, and sleep a few winks. A twelve-inch-wide bronze plate with grooves along the top was fastened to the aft cockpit coaming. We made a metal fin that would fit over the tiller and nestle in the teeth of the bronze plate, thus keeping the tiller in one spot. Rubber shock cord was wrapped around the tiller and fitted to cleats on deck. This way, I hoped, the boat could hold her course when I was not available.

She was rigged with six sails for all manner of weather—a mainsail that could be reefed smaller in strong winds, a large genoa for light air, a medium jib for moderate winds, a storm trysail and twin genoas with whisker poles for running before the trade winds. These twins were specifically designed so I wouldn't have to venture on the fore deck. I was supposed to be able to raise the sails, top the poles, trim the foreguys and afterguys, lower the sails, and lower the poles and secure them—all from my nest in the cockpit.

Winches were installed on the cabin top for hauling on halyards and topping lifts; two more were placed on the coaming within easy reach of the helm. In all, eighteen lines led to the cockpit, eighteen lines that I would maneuver to determine our fate.

And for all these items, there were back-ups. Anything aboard that could break or be lost required a replacement or substitute. I couldn't allow myself to be stuck out there without the appropriate equipment and gear. And I, the sole voyager on this mission, would learn to fix my way through any possible problem I could imagine on the open sea.

Tools became my buddies in arms—pliers, screw drivers, wrenches, hammer, cable cutters, metal saw, wood saw, hand drill, screws, bolts, clamps, marlin line, sealing compounds, and so much more. Just about anything you'll find in a handyman's truck. I even brought snorkeling gear in case I had to patch a hole in the hull.

I was lucky to have such a reliable traveling mate, a boat that could weather the troubles that lay ahead. "The worse it gets, the better she likes it." That's what Gundrun Reineth would come to say of the Folkboat in *Rudder* magazine, and oh, how right he was. "The boat is so good it makes even a mediocre helmsman look good." By the time Reineth's statement was printed in June 1966, a year after my voyage, I could attest first-hand to his accuracy.

But the boat was only half the equation; I was the second half. My body, my rhythms. I had to change my whole way of living, everything I thought and ate and did from the moment I woke each morning. I had to learn new routines and divorce myself from life, from everything but sailing.

And I had to get in shape, so as often as possible, I tackled both tasks at once. I sanded and varnished the hull and discovered muscles I had long forgotten. I hoisted myself to the top of the mast in a boatswain's chair, sanding on the way up and varnishing on the way down. I was shoved into the water, fully clothed, and learned to pull myself up again. At night I set my alarm for the wee hours of morning, forcing myself to break my normal sleep patterns. I had to endure such crazy schemes. Out at sea anything could happen at any hour, and I knew I would sustain many sleepless nights.

Beyond all that, I had to learn how to get where I was going.

I got a phone call one day. "What are you doing about your navigation?" It was Division Chief Hugh McDonald calling from the Los Angeles County Sheriff's Department. He had heard of my impending quest through the sailing grapevine. "Maybe we'd better get together on my boat and talk about it," he suggested. Good thing, too, because I hadn't a clue about navigation before he called. Hugh was a master navigator. He was a licensed helicopter pilot. He wanted to help me out.

When we first met aboard Hugh's private boat, his wife was there. In truth, she was there to "check me out," as Hugh later confided. My wits, my motivation, my sanity—whether anything seemed askew. If I was a nut, Hugh wanted to know before he invested too much time in me.

I must have passed inspection because my navigation lessons started on the spot. More jargon: latitude, longitude, declination, azimuth, and zenith distance. Greenwich mean time, zone time, apparent time, and watch time. I learned to work four instruments: the compass, which gives your direction; the taffrail log, with a dial face and turning hands to register distance traveled; the chronometer, a watch in gimbals, for keeping precise time; and the sextant, for measuring the angle of sun and stars from the horizon. With these, I could determine my fix, my exact latitude and longitude at any given time.

Beyond gadgets, I learned all about dead reckoning, the distance traveled on each compass course. It's a critical concept, dead reckoning; it tells you where you think you are. It's an estimation of the boat's position, using your compass and log, the wind, the current, the time. Yet it's not good enough because waves and currents and drifts, over hours and days, will lead you astray. A solo sailor, back in the days before global positioning systems (GPS), was never exactly where she believed herself to be.

By day, I stood at the end of Venice pier, taking sights of the sun. By twilight, I studied by "shooting" the stars, navigating by the heavens. My head was so crammed with navigation, I studied it in my dreams. It's a blessing I always had a knack for math. Hugh gave me little exercises on paper, and I furiously worked through them, my mind churning out calculations. Sometimes it didn't work. Sometimes I ended up in Arizona or Death Valley and we'd chuckle—good thing I was still sailing on paper, or I'd have been left dry on a desert plain.

Hugh was the most remarkable man I had ever met. He was a man of myriad talents, a man of flair, an author of many books. I have four of his documentary novels. The books about Hugh describe a life made for the movies: During World War II, he was in the Office of Strategic Services, which became the CIA. He spent years behind the iron curtain and escaped by crossing the Hungarian border disguised as a member of a circus troupe. He invented the Identikit, used in making composite pictures of crime suspects. He was head of Barry Goldwater's security during his run for the White House. And he was the first pilot chosen to fly the infamous U-2 spy plane, but he declined, telling President Eisenhower the Russians had the capability to shoot down the plane. (Francis Gary Powers was then asked to fly the mission and was shot down near Sverdlovsk and convicted of espionage.)

Hugh was a devout Catholic. His wife later told me how Hugh lit a candle every morning in church, wherever they were, during a cross-country road trip they took while I was at sea.

By the end of the third week of navigation training, Hugh looked at me and said, "That's it. You can go anywhere in the world you want." Not only would I pinpoint Honolulu, he said, I could find any charted speck of land in the ocean. Yet the preparations didn't end: my body needed attending and mending. My personal friend and physician, Dr. Ralph Gold, gave me a thorough physical that I passed with ease. With time and insight and great care, he put together a first-aid kit befitting several months at sea, stocking me with antibiotics, antiseptics, splints, bandages, and tourniquet. There were pills for stomachache, earache, back pain, muscle pain. Pills for keeping me awake or putting me to sleep. Aspirin, eye drops, cough syrup, and codeine. High-potency vitamins and extensive instructions regarding symptoms, dosage, and treatment. I would be the only doctor on board. I would need to be ready for anything from a headache to a broken arm.

With all his preparation, Dr. Gold thought me reasonably ready for sea. Only one question continued to worry him after my voyage began: what would I do with a burst appendix? Thank heavens it turned out to be a nonissue; and by the next time I would meet him with another kooky idea, four years later, he would have an answer for me.

I began preparing the boat for emergencies. A radar reflector was devised from plywood and aluminum foil. It would spin with the wind and reflect the sunlight brilliantly, improving my profile in any ship's radar. It would allow passing ships to locate me or avoid me, whichever was better.

I taped a cheat sheet of Morse code messages to the hanging

locker door, in case I needed aid. If a passing ship or plane were to spot me, I could blink out messages with my spotlight or signaling mirror. Also tacked to that door was a calendar, each day to be crossed off so I would never miscalculate my navigation. I would use that calendar religiously; I would never remember time on my own. The mind plays too many tricks.

My vessel was nearly ready but it still had no name. Then one day while I was varnishing, Al came along. "My, but that looks sharp," he said.

"She'll soon be ready for sea."

And there it was: *Sea Sharp*, the perfect name for a woman who had grown up practicing the cello two hours a day. I designed and sewed the boat's house flag, five parallel white waves on a heavy, blue canvas background with a golden C eighth note and a sharp on the staff. A seagull in flight represented the flag of the eighth note. C Sharp. *Sea Sharp*. My boat was properly tagged for the journey.

Everything was coming together. Yet in the ten weeks of *Sea Sharp*'s metamorphosis, I couldn't take her out for a sail. In fact, I had never been offshore alone—ever—and my departure date was just a few weeks away.

I was strongly urged to get off land—sail somewhere, anywhere, and quickly! So I prepared for a two-day trip up the coast to Point Dume and then across the channel to Anacapa Island, where the winds were supposed to be stronger and the currents rougher. My friend Dione Patton had never been sailing, but she volunteered for the ride. We packed sleeping bags and foul-weather gear, loaded the boat with food and drink, and set out on our merry course. Good winds whisked us to Point Dume, and all was moving well at four knots. Then it wasn't. The sun dropped as we headed toward Anacapa and the wind fell flat. The sea turned glassy, and there we sat with limp sails, smack in the middle of the shipping lanes. That was not the place to be. I had been warned of potential disaster in the night: freighters and tankers chugging past us in the dark, nearly running us down, missing our dim little running lights.

So there we bobbed, sleepless and drifting all through the night, shining spotlights on our sails so the passing ships could see us. The crewmen of a much-too-close ship barraged us with catcalls, and we had no recourse but to sit and smile and hope for wind.

By sunrise, sixteen ships had passed us before a small breeze finally took hold and pushed us along. We sailed the entire day, slowly making our way home, arriving in port well overdue at midnight. No doubt, an inauspicious first attempt at mastering the sea. It was little inspiration to those who already doubted my sanity. But I persisted.

Many speculated that I would never make it; others speculated I wouldn't really go, that I would turn around in a few days' time. Some guessed I'd simply disappear. I let the speculators speculate while I stuck to my course as planned. I was determined. I was willing to pay the price. Without obstacles, I told myself, there is no need for courage.

I wrote a letter to the Eleventh District United States Coast Guard Office, a courtesy simply informing them of my plans. The coast guard didn't like my idea. They thanked me for the information on my intended crossing. They likewise informed me that the movement of vessels within Marina del Rey, and the entrance channel thereto, fell under the cognizance of the harbormaster, who had been furnished a copy of my letter. They told me that safety is a matter of deep concern to the coast guard and that they would be remiss in not advising me that they considered my intended voyage extremely hazardous. They recommended I abandon my plans. They informed me (the letter was full of informing) that should I or my boat become disabled during the journey, my survival would depend on the unlikely possibility of a passing vessel discovering me and my plight. They informed me, due to the great distance involved and a lack of marine radio equipment, an air search would be fruitless. The letter was signed, "sincerely yours," by a captain of the U.S. Coast Guard and chief of the Search and Rescue Branch. It was written by direction of the coast guard district commander.

Well. I suppose it was a logical reply. And they had every right to warn me. But they certainly didn't change my mind.

I proceeded as planned; there was much to be done. Space was at a prime on *Sea Sharp*, just twenty-five feet long and five feet wide with a cabin that had room enough to sit but never stand. She had a ten-inch stainless steel sink in the galley with a freshwater hand pump.

Food, water, sails, tools, surplus gear, life raft, toiletries, cameras, clothes, foul-weather gear, tool chest, first-aid kit, spare parts, cabin lamp, and kerosene for the running lights—where to store it all? I had to map my belongings carefully. I diagrammed the boat and planned everything to the inch, with weight distributed evenly and items stashed in meticulous order so I could easily find the supplies I needed when I needed them.

If you think packing for an airplane trip is tricky, try stowing a boat for a crossing that could take ninety days. A painstaking ordeal, to be sure, everything must be thought out and stashed in such a manner that things I needed first would be on top and things I used every day would be easy to reach. Weight had to be distributed evenly around the boat at all times. And the items I hoped never to need were stashed in the back, the bottom, or hard-to-reach places. The chronometer, sextant, and Zenith transoceanic shortwave radio had to be kept dry and secure; a sudden roll couldn't be allowed to jar them loose. *Sea Sharp* had a hanging storage locker sixteen inches wide, but no drawers or cupboards.

Two sleeping bunks had storage space below. I removed two extra bunks and cushions from the forepeak, making more room for stashing sails and provisions.

The bilge—a big, empty area in the bottom of the boat beneath the cabin—would seem a natural place to store gear, except that sea water would seep in regularly. Even so, I could store canned foods there. That meant I had to remove each label, mark each can with grease pencil, and dip the cans in lacquer to prevent rusting. I threw a lacquering party, and my friends pitched in to help. I packed a well-balanced mix of meats, fruits, and vegetables in small cans since I didn't want leftovers. I wanted to make sure I knew what I was eating, so without labels or pictures, the grease pencil was essential. Otherwise the contents of each can would be a mystery. What if I grabbed beets for breakfast? Vegetables in the morning—not for me. Plain cans with no color and no pictures proved to be very unappetizing. I would learn that food had the power to make or break my mood. Those little cans had enormous psychological clout.

I carried provisions for ninety days. As Al put it: "What if you were to miss the island? Your next landfall might be Samoa or New Guinea." I should be prepared. A quart of water a day is sufficient for human consumption. All my water was treated with halazone purification tablets to keep it from going bad. I would use fresh water for nothing but drinking and cooking. *Sea Sharp*'s built-in water tank held ten gallons, so I bought twenty-six one-gallon plastic jugs and stowed them individually. That way, I wouldn't lose my entire water supply if one container were to spring a leak. Plus, I could distribute the weight evenly around the boat and shuffle the containers as I emptied them.

There was so much more to bring! I had an Avon four-man life raft with CO_2 cartridges to inflate it, sectional oars, and a mast for a small sail. This came courtesy of Seagull Marine Products in Los Angeles, a gift to my cause. I filled a waterproof duffel bag with lifeboat provisions and water for twenty-one days. I added a patching kit, hand bellows, and a canopy to block the sun. Fishing line, tackle, knife, dye marker, shark repellent, waterproof flashlight, signaling mirror, hand compass, small plastic sextant, navigation almanac, can opener as well as so many tools I hoped never to use, all requiring precious space on the boat.

There was something else I had to fit aboard: Sarah Beth-Ann. She was my tiny pet turtle, a freshwater species from Thailand. I couldn't leave her at home, so I invited her along. I bought her a small aquarium to fit in the galley sink and I made her a little harness to fit around her shell, which would allow her to roam the boat without being washed overboard.

I had never owned a camera, didn't know how to expose a picture, didn't know how to meter the light—more lessons. I learned to use three different cameras, still and moving. I bought a German Zeiss Ikon with easy settings, built-in light meter, and wide-angle lens. Nothing automatic in those days. I borrowed a 35 mm underwater camera with a clamp, which I could secure to numerous spots around the boat. With a string attached to the shutter release, I could photograph myself in action. In addition I borrowed a 16 mm movie camera with wide-angle and telephoto lenses, which I would hold by hand. It fastened to a tripod, and with a two-way pulley, I could capture my chores on film. Through the workings of all three cameras, I would have a visual record of my voyage.

People asked me why I wasn't taking a radiotelephone. Weight was an issue, and so was the perpetual dampness. Already, the boat was stuffed to the railings with provisions. And a radio wasn't just a radio then; it would require batteries, a generator, and gas. All total, it would add two hundred pounds to the boat. A twenty-five-watt radiophone could call within a twenty-five-mile radius; what were the odds of another vessel being within twenty-five miles if I were in trouble? In the end, a radiotelephone simply wasn't worth its weight or my while, yet my critics couldn't understand that.

Departure time drew nearer and could no longer be measured in weeks but in days. People asked whether I was scared, but I was too busy to feel fear. Deep down, I felt calm. I slept well. If I hadn't believed I could do it, I wouldn't have attempted such a journey. I was not going to lose myself on purpose, as some skeptics speculated; nor did I simply want to be alone, as others presumed. To the contrary—loneliness was a demon I would learn to face and overcome.

Besides my trip to sea, I had to arrange my life on land. I asked my landlord to care for my garden, and I paid rent for ten weeks in advance, which would cover my crossing as well as three weeks in Hawaii. I arranged for a friend to start my car occasionally and pick up mail. I was realistic; I updated my will. The week before departure, my minister dedicated that Sunday's services to me and asked the congregation for their prayers.

Just fourteen weeks passed between the day I bought my boat and my departure for Hawaii. Eight months total experience. And with that, I hoped I was suitably ready for a run to Hawaii.

The First Sail

M y scheduled departure time was June 12 at noon. There were reasons for this. I couldn't put it off forever, couldn't afford more time without a job. June and July were months of favorable weather, and by leaving on that date I would have two full moons to brighten my nights at sea. I also knew that July 4 would mark the start of the biannual Transpacific Yacht Race from Los Angeles to Honolulu. While I was to sail alone, hundreds of others would be making the same route in teams. They might spot me along the way and report my progress, and that thought consoled me.

My venture gained celebrity as the date drew close. Strangers met me at the docks, curious about my trip, curious about the woman who thought it up. Several men offered to accompany me; I declined, of course. They meant well, but they obviously didn't understand.

"Is it true?" a stranger called to ask me early one morning about a month before my departure. "That you're planning to sail to Honolulu?" He was a reporter with the *Los Angeles Herald Examiner*.

"Yes."

"But you're not going alone, are you? That's what I heard."

"Oh, yes I am."

He wanted an interview. He wanted to know what everyone else wanted to know—why and how, and where on earth had this idea come from?

I had never put my feelings into words. I didn't have to explain these things to other sailors; they already understood. Others simply thought I was nuts and didn't ask questions. So when the reporter asked me, "Why?" I didn't know what to say.

"Has any woman ever done it before?" he asked.

I didn't have an answer for that either. It had never occurred to me that I might be the first, but it turned out I was, a fact I wouldn't learn until months later. It took a reporter to tell me. I didn't know or care before my departure.

Being the first had nothing to do with my plans and had never figured in my thinking. I simply wanted to sail to Hawaii alone and didn't see why I couldn't.

The next day the *Herald Examiner* story was printed; "Secretary's Dream Trip," sprawled across half a page. I never went looking for publicity, but there it was. I was more than just a gutsy girl from Prineville, Oregon, now. Reporters called me day and night for twenty-three days straight, from the time that story ran until my departure day. Photographers found me in the harbor. The Associated Press, United Press International, cbs from Francisco—they all found me. Within days, all seven Los Angeles television stations had me on the news. Radio reporters followed me home, and all this fuss nearly brought my work on the boat to a halt.

Without my knowledge or approval, the *Herald Examiner* story invited the public to see the boat the following Sunday and suggested each visitor bring a can of provisions. Suffice it to say, the traffic jam at Marina del Rey that Sunday was horrendous. The line stretched for hours, all those people hoping to greet me. I must have shaken all the right hands in Los Angeles—and a few of the left. Eleven hundred people in all signed my guest book, with all manner of farewells: "Have fun. . . . Good luck. . . . Fair winds. . . . God be with you. . . . You'll make it. . . . Don't look back." And a skeptic or two: "See you in eight days."

The crowd had read the stories, heard the news, and the people came loaded with goods. There were canned foods, condiments, powdered milk, soft drinks, soap, and tissue. There was turtle food for Sarah Beth-Ann, a bottle of champagne, a bottle of brandy. All that caboodle nearly sank the dock.

One woman brought a wishbone wrapped in red satin. She called it "God's piece," an Aztec family tradition handed down from her grandmother. In her family, when a relative embarked on a journey, she would wrap up a wishbone for good luck. The little talisman was meant to tell Mother Earth that I sailed with God and should be spared all harm.

One man brought me a six-pack of Coke. I had no idea why. He just asked that I drink the Coke but save the bottles for a man who would meet me in Honolulu. I love a good mystery, so I obliged.

Another man handed me a taste test. He supplied me with ten days of dehydrated foods—meats, vegetables, fruits, cereals, desserts, and milk shakes. All new products on the market; he wanted an evaluation from sea.

All that stuff filled my apartment kitchen with stacks of food four feet high. Elmer Peterson, an NBC reporter, stopped by one day and he could barely maneuver his gear through that maze. No way would I ever need so much food aboard the boat.

In the final days of preparation, my dearest friends threw me a party, and I would learn weeks later that I needed their memory to survive. I could subsist on the sheer words of people who believed in my voyage. Their thoughts would push me through the roughest waters. I would read and reread and reread again all those messages in my logbook: "Our love and best wishes, our pride and our prayers ride with you," they told me. "Some people have mountains that need climbing—you happen to have an ocean that needs crossing," they encouraged. "You really are the captain of your ship and the master of your soul." They made me laugh, too: "I said it to Christopher, I said it to Wilbur and Orville, now I say it to you—take up stamp collecting!"

Among all those wise and witty words, one friend's assessment of my voyage struck the essence of my soul: "Everyone has their own craft to sail. There have been seas you have already weathered, alone, squalls you have gone through, alone, rough waters you have already battled and won, alone. It is for this reason you can and will make this trip all the way, though at times there may be doubt. Bless you, but now, as always, come through."

The day before departure, all was snug inside the boat, everything but my toothbrush and makeup case. My shore clothes were packed in a suitcase and waiting to be flown ahead to Hawaii when the time arrived.

I dined that night with friends at a rooftop restaurant with a view to the glistening lights of Los Angeles, a thousand beacons of civilization, that community. It was my last night amid the masses. The boat was ready. I was ready.

We drove then to the marina and watched *Sea Sharp* among all the other boats. I kept thinking of my lessons, dos and don'ts, the mechanics of a boat and her sails.

Just a few hours remained, and until then I hadn't thought about the burden I was handing my friends. I was their responsibility. They believed in me; I knew that. But I also knew they dreaded my leaving, too. They had delivered me to that dock, had prepared my mind, and had cared for my soul. That night, for the first time, I saw my responsibility to them: to return.

June 12, 1965, dawned gray and foggy. I woke fully rested and tiptoed into the shower for my last hot-water shampoo. I cooked my last breakfast on an electric stove, and I thought of a dry house, sockets, and switches that make things happen, all the comforts we take for granted.

That morning I wore new sailing clothes, white slacks and a navy blazer. I arrived at the marina, which was all hustle and bustle, full of people ogling *Sea Sharp* with her cover rolled back. There in the crowd were my minister, my banker, my doctor, co-workers, neighbors, friends, and so many strangers. My beautiful boat tugged at her mooring lines, just as anxious for the start as I.

A fleet was set to see me off, and I had arranged for friends to tag along awhile. Al would tow me to the breakwater on a fifty-foot racing sloop, *Cotton Blossom II*, with seven of my closest friends. They would sail beside me the first day until we parted, for better or worse.

The commodore of the International Yachtsman's Exchange Club presented me with a mission, a letter from Los Angeles Mayor Samuel Yorty, which I was to take to Mayor Neal Blaisdell in Honolulu. Of course, Mayor Yorty told me, "There are faster ways of delivering the mail. But none are nearly so romantic or adventurous."

More gifts arrived, some with practical inclinations: lemons "for scurvy" and a can of octopus tentacles for "more hands." The crowd bombarded me with questions, but there were two that I will never forget: "Will you stop along the way?" and "Will you anchor every night?"

For the record, the only land between California's offshore islands and Hawaii would be fifteen thousand feet beneath *Sea Sharp*'s bottom. I'd have little chance to stop or anchor.

At 11:55 that morning, *Cotton Blossom II* eased up to my slip and threw me a towline. *Sea Sharp*'s dock lines were removed for the last time and readied for stowage; I wouldn't be needing them for many weeks. Tears and hugs went all around. The towline was secured and we—Sarah Beth-Ann, *Sea Sharp*, and I—abandoned land. The figures on the dock shrank as we weaved through the harbor. Horns, whistles, bells, cameras, and waving hands, all growing smaller and smaller, and quieter, until they were gone.

As we approached the breakwater at the harbor entrance, I raised the genoa and trimmed the mainsail. We were astonishingly heavy in the water but I didn't worry. Our load would lighten as I ate and drank my way along. The sails filled in an offshore breeze, and I cast off the towline. I set my course for Catalina with a fleet of press boats and spectators following for more than an hour until they, too, began to fade. By midafternoon I could see blips of sails on the horizon behind, but only *Cotton Blossom II* and *Sea Sharp* moved together.

So there I was on water. I had work to do. I set the tiller to maintain course and went below. I changed from my pretty blue and white clothes to jeans and sweatshirt; my departure suit would be stowed until I reached shore. I stored the dock lines and checked that all provisions were riding snugly. Then I settled down to a Dodgers game on the radio and called back and forth to my friends on *Cotton Blossom II*. I wasn't quite alone yet.

Catalina's outline lay ahead as dusk appeared in its first pink rays. The winds calmed as we neared the island, and by 8:00 p.m. the sea was smooth without a ripple. "How about putting into a sheltered cove, getting a good night's sleep and an early start in the morning?" Al called to me. I wouldn't sleep two winks as it was, drifting toward a rocky shore, so I agreed. Al anchored *Cotton Blossom II*, I tied *Sea Sharp* alongside, and we all enjoyed dinner on deck before sleeping. My first night aboard *Sea Sharp*, I was lulled by gentle swells, snug and protected. It would not happen again for a long time.

After the sun rose and I ate a hot breakfast, I was ready to forge my own way. This time, the tears were in my eyes as I bade farewell to friends. I raised the sails and set a course to round the east end of San Clemente Island, another twenty-eight miles, before leaving all sight of land behind.

"See you in Honolulu," Al called to me. They grew smaller and smaller in the distance. *Cotton Blossom II* was but a speck on the horizon, then gone. That was it. I was alone.

But not for long. That afternoon, I had the company of a military jet that circled low three times. The pilot blinked a light, dipped his wings, then disappeared. It would be my last visit for a while.

The hours wore on with another Dodgers game on the radio while I planned a daily routine. I would need to mark my navigation log every six hours for dead reckoning. The kerosene running lights would need wiping and filling every day. I needed to pump the bilge, check the lines, clean seaweed from the rotator on the taffrail log, and continually check for leaks.

I didn't see the island of San Clemente until almost dark that second day. I made a thermos of hot coffee, tucked a sleeping bag into the cockpit, and made ready for the night. I knew I shouldn't sleep with land off my starboard bow—still too dangerous—so I trimmed the sails and set the tiller to steer well offshore. I thought I would merely rest, but the last I remember was the radio playing at 1:30 a.m. I must have conked out after that. The Lord had his hand on the tiller that night, because when I awoke at sunrise, *Sea Sharp* had rounded the island. Her bow was pointed toward Honolulu on the course I had intended, with none of my supervision.

Day three started gray and heavy. I made fresh coffee and opened a can of apricot juice, but I still wasn't hungry. For the rest of the trip, all my tea and coffee went into a thermos so as not to waste a single drop of fresh water. When the leftover coffee turned cold, I used it to brush my teeth. Brown and bitter, but it worked.

The sun was nowhere in sight when it came time for my first

sextant shot. The breeze stayed light but the swells increased and stronger winds lay ahead. I wanted to be prepared, so I went on deck to reef the mainsail, reducing its area and size by a third. As *Sea Sharp* tossed and rolled in the morphing seas, I grew sick, so early in the journey. Because of all the hubbub surrounding my departure had zapped my appetite, I hadn't been eating, so my retching came up dry. I hobbled to the cockpit with dread: Would every day at sea be like this? Weak and shaky, stomach in cramps? There was no way I could endure that for forty days.

Despite my handicap, the winds grew to thirty miles per hour and we flew through the water that afternoon. But *Sea Sharp* wouldn't stick to her course more than fifteen minutes with weather increasing. What could I do? "Don't look back," someone had written in my guestbook before I departed. It was good advice. I plowed ahead. With nightfall, the air calmed and I slept in twenty-minute spurts, my mind still occupied with the self-steering issue. "Whenever you face a problem, think it through," the voice of Hugh, my navigation guru, rang in my head. "Make it make sense."

By morning I had conceived a logical plan. The boat continually changed course because there wasn't enough play in the rudder. To fix this, I used my hacksaw to remove some of the teeth from the bronze plate, thereby allowing more movement. This project took me nearly a day. A small assignment on land magnifies at sea, where the footing sways and every movement is twice the trouble. But my plan worked—the rudder worked better and *Sea Sharp* kept her way.

From then on she would hold course for maybe an hour at a time, but never as well as I had hoped. It wasn't until I reached the trade winds, when the twin gennys allowed me to go many hours without steering *Sea Sharp* myself.

Once I had fixed the rudder and stabilized my course, my hunger returned. I had eaten almost nothing since departing two days earlier. Friends had left me fried chicken for the ride, but it had already spoiled. Instead, I heated a can of stew on the Sterno stove and ate straight from the tin, in order to save water on dishwashing. I could never use water without thinking it through. By journey's end, I would be obsessed with water and the idea of its consumption. Never again could I turn on a faucet with indifference.

The next day broke dismal and foggy again, and I grew dismayed. Hugh had planned on flying out in a two-engine Apache just to say hi. But a thick blanket blocked the sky, and I knew our little rendezvous wouldn't happen. Even if he could fly, he'd never find me. Still, I watched for signs. I stretched my ears for the distant growl of a small plane. Had he circled the sea and missed me? Did he worry? I wished we could talk, but I had no answers out there on my boat, no conversation to share. Weeks later I would learn that Hugh had flown to San Clemente Island then turned back in a fog, reporting that "finding a needle in a haystack would be easier."

I grew lonesome when the wind died. It would always be that way, a sluggish ride giving me too much time to think. I'd listen to the radio and write in my diary, while the hours would stagger on. I'd slip Sarah Beth-Ann into her harness and let her slink around deck, such as a turtle could. She didn't like a pitching boat and the salt-water spray, so she only came out in the calm. She wasn't eating much, and I started to worry. Seasickness? In a turtle?

By the fifth day, the sky beamed with sunshine, raising my spirits. I tuned the radio midmorning to KABC news.

"She'll make it. She's a very spunky gal." It was Al on the radio. I was tickled to hear that voice, which somehow verified my existence. But not every morning brought sweet words to my ears. On that same station a while later, the moderator asked the audience,

"What do you think of that woman making the trip to Hawaii by herself?"

"She's just a frustrated woman running away," one caller replied.

Oh, the nerve. I went on with business, finding small pleasures in the world around me, drenched in sunlight. That man on the radio didn't know me in the least.

Once, while heating lunch, I heard an engine drone. I peeked my head from the cockpit and saw a military plane approaching from the stern at low altitude. It circled four times, so close I saw two men waving. That was it, a quick apparition to break the scene.

A warm, dry spell continued, so I shed heavy clothes and stripped for my first oceanside bath. I worked myself into a good lather, then doused myself in buckets of seawater, icy cold but it felt so good. I wasn't washing clothes on this journey. Instead, I had packed hand-me-downs and old worn-out togs; and when they were thoroughly grimy, I pitched them overboard, leaving a trail of dirty laundry. I know, I know, I was a litterbug! But everything went overboard in those pre-eco days. As I tossed a red plaid shirt, I laughed to myself. I had a vision of a shark swimming straight into that shirt, making it the best-dressed shark at sea.

Even at sea a woman's work is never done. Calm hours meant housekeeping time. I had two goals: to keep *Sea Sharp* as sharp as her name and to keep myself fresh and feminine. Every chance I could, I washed the salts off her topsides and polished her stanchions, pulpits, and winches. These chores were easy when sailing on agreeable seas. The clear evenings were gifts to enjoy, with sunsets of brilliance in myriad shades of yellow, purple, and pink. I couldn't tear myself away from the tiller, but I was fortunate to have a hand on the steering and both eyes on the grandeur.

At dusk each evening, I would light the kerosene lamp in the cabin and I'd write. The diary kept my mind intact. Writing became my sole communication, a conversation of one that comforted me in moody times. But the penmanship looked nothing like mine; it reflected the rocking of the boat, as though I scribbled from the saddle of a horse in full canter. It's an odd thing to see one's own thoughts and words in an unknown script that is nearly illegible.

I made sure to write plenty. When you're crossing the sea, you have to write down everything you do because your mind no longer remembers, not properly. You don't recall what you have done or haven't done because the mind misses the temporal benchmarks of land. You don't remember the last time you washed your hair. You don't know when the sail went overboard. It all has to be written down, every task of every day; and when you flip through your log, you are shocked at what your mind is telling you. Your mind is telling you that you showered an hour ago when, really, it's been two days.

I made friends as we cruised along, a contingent of gooney birds that followed my wake. I love those birds. A gooney is an albatross with broad wings that soars for hours, barely skimming the tops of waves, disappearing into the troughs of the sea. It is not graceful when landing on water, webbed feet outstretched, stiff legs plowing through the surface. Takeoff is funnier yet, as though the bird is running atop the ocean, hoping for speed enough to launch its gangly little body. Rarely does the gooney reach land except to mate. But it will trail a boat hundreds of miles, waiting for handouts, waiting for friends like me.

My gooneys had competition from a man-o'-war, a bird with a small body but gigantic wingspan four or five feet across. The bird glides gracefully, then dives for food. I watched one circle hundreds of feet high before a steep plummet to the surface, where it pried a fish from the clutches of a gooney.

The prettiest birds were the sea swallows with soft, white feathers, red feet and legs, and long straight bills. They flew close to the rigging, trying to land on *Sea Sharp*'s mast, playing games with me.

One evening while marking my chart in the cabin, a great splashing and chattering erupted outside. I emerged to find the boat surrounded by thousands of sardines. They swam in circles, a cyclone of fish beneath me and around me, everywhere I could see. Suddenly, shoals of skipjack tuna plowed forward in a sardine feeding frenzy. The sardines were followed by hundreds of screeching birds arriving from all directions. The sea boiled with excitement, the air buzzed with the hunt, and we floated in the center of commotion. I stood for an hour, just watching.

Then the hubbub died and the sea was still, just like that, in an eerie way that signals danger. A seven-foot shadow rose from the depths. The shark glided slowly, baring its fin to the sun, brushing *Sea Sharp*'s side—so close. I could see him eating ravenously, feasting on sardines. This was survival of the fittest in its truest form.

For two days during my second week, the sea stood in a dead calm. It's hard to imagine the gaping ocean as a glassy mirror, but that's what it became. I amused myself as best I could, to kill the hours of no sailing. I tied a string to a paper plate and filled it with food for the birds, pulling them closer to the boat as they ate.

What a foolish oversight, not to have brought books for the journey. I had figured I wouldn't have time to read. Someone on the dock had handed me a paperback, the only book aboard. I stashed it on a shelf in the hanging locker. Such temptation, but so many days lay ahead. I would save that single book until I could no longer resist; I didn't even peek at the title. It turned into a mental game. I knew I would need it more tomorrow, and even more the day after that. So instead, I pulled the newspaper packing from around the sextant in the life raft—it was the February 12 legal notices of Richmond, California, which provided precisely zero minutes of riveting reading. Next page: obituaries.

Nothing changed the next morning. I awoke to water so calm that the tin cans and paper bowl from my previous night's dinner were floating beside the boat (Yes, garbage, like laundry, went to sea in those days). My rubbish hadn't moved an inch, and neither had I. How would I make it to Honolulu if I couldn't even beat my garbage?

The calm remained until my tenth evening at sea, when I spotted a little ripple stirring on still water. "I moved a few feet in a little gust!" I exclaimed to my diary. My limp sails finally swelled, and we started to make steerageway. It was a crawl, but it was movement. "Make the boat go," Hugh's voice called to me. I tried my best.

Ten days had passed, and I had traveled just 364 miles. A paltry record. People would think I didn't know how to sail, and maybe they were right. Before leaving land a sailor named Frank climbed aboard *Sea Sharp* and told me of his expedition the previous summer. He had sailed his eighteen-footer to Hawaii alone. It took him fifty-one days, a good ten days longer than I had hoped to sail. But now I began to wonder if I'd make it in two months.

Such thoughts made me lonely, longing for companions. I spotted the smokestack of a distant ship, but it came nowhere near. It slipped over the horizon and away from me. Through the weeks ahead, I would see many little specks out there, but no one ever stopped to say hi.

I thought of people who have undergone isolation experiments, but their aloneness was different from mine. They had known where they were and how long confinement would last. They had had the option of leaving. True, I was on the ocean of my own free will, but no one knew where I was exactly. And I knew that no one knew. I couldn't break free from that isolation. I could end my journey by jumping into the sea, or I could sail on through. I was the only one privy to my thoughts along the way. How often I wished to take a long walk; how I wished *Sea Sharp* were twenty-six feet instead of twenty-five so I might enjoy the pleasure of one extra step.

And yet, I never seriously thought of turning back. Not really.

June 23, day 12, it was the most satisfying day of the trip to that point. The wind pushed us steadily at three knots. My navigation fix at noon showed us at 28°1'N, 121°34'W. The sea sparkled deep blue—every ripple, a diamond. *Sea Sharp* threw up a spray—each drop, a gem in the sun. I was thoroughly at peace.

I sat in the cockpit eating a can of spaghetti and meatballs when a thunderous whoosh startled me to my feet. Spaghetti splattered everywhere. Not fifty feet away was a whale, trailing beside me for twenty minutes, spouting great gasps. I guessed it was about thirty-five feet, a full ten feet longer than *Sea Sharp*. It crossed in front of the bow, causing *Sea Sharp* to feel its wake as it left us behind. What a sight to relish—if only I had had someone to share it with.

The winds stayed steady, and I awoke to another clear morning on June 24. *Sea Sharp* ploughed through the sea, a friend with the wind. We had covered seventy-one miles in twenty-four hours, our best run yet. I made coffee in the cabin, feeling cheery and bright, but my mood spun on a moment. Sarah Beth-Ann lay dead. After days of low appetite and lethargy, she had conked out on me.

Her death was a jarring loss. She had been my friend and comrade, and I prepared to give her a proper burial at sea. I swaddled her in white cloth, placed her on a board from the hatchway, and covered her with my yacht ensign. With a silent prayer, I slid her into the sea and dropped her aquarium overboard. I mourned my turtle. But her death meant something beyond the loss of a friend: with no more Sarah Beth-Ann, I was fully alone.

FOUR

Storm

The mind is most troublesome in the worst of winds, be they dead or furious—and for sailors, the worst of winds are either.

It was noon during the end of my second week at sea, and the sky loomed black and ominous. The winds blew stronger, the clouds turned grayer. I knew it was better to reach my destination safely than to race against time; other sailors had warned me of this. Better to reduce sail too soon rather than too late. If I waited too long, I might jeopardize the mast or rigging. I knew the mainsail and genoa jib had to come down, but I pushed my limits. What joy to fly along at four knots. I was behind schedule; here was my wind. I used it as long as I could.

With winds at twenty-five miles per hour and just a scintilla of daylight left, *Sea Sharp* and I settled down for some serious sailing. I'd never flown through water so fast. The sea broke over the deck and rushed the cockpit. Whitecaps crested all around me.

I was cold, dressed in jeans, sweatshirt, heavy jacket, foul-weather gear, and rubber boots. I cradled a thermos of hot coffee and stashed five concentrated food bars and two candy bars in one pocket and a bottle of Ritalin pills in another. A tempest stirred, and I knew I faced a treacherous night.

I secured the radio in the galley sink by wedging it into place with pieces of foam rubber. Anything breakable aboard was padded and fastened tightly. Darkness fell fast, but I would have no sleep that night. I lit the lamp, scrambled on deck, and sealed the cabin below.

That night was the darkest I'd yet endured, pure black; but we charged through near zero visibility as though a starship making its way through space. I could hear Al, "Be good to the boat and give it the easiest ride possible." Any sensible sailor would have admonished me for not reducing sail that night, but I was on a roll. *Sea Sharp* shuddered from bow to stern with every wave; I felt like we were airborne.

But the thrill fizzled as I knew it would, and fear took the helm. I had two options: I could continue at breakneck speed or I could attempt to lower my sails in darkness. I did nothing. I simply held forth as the hours dragged, in anticipation of dawn. I didn't know what time it was, but I knew eventually light would return. I hid in the cockpit, thinking. And then I remembered: a fisherman's reef!

I strapped the genoa as tightly as I could and eased the main to a luff. The wind consequently drove into the backside of the mainsail, diminishing the efficiency of both sails and cutting my speed. A quick glance at the clock told me the sun would rise about thirty minutes later. I chose to ride the storm out through the remainder of the darkness.

When morning came, I had to get those sails down. I hadn't slept, but Ritalin and anxiety had kept me going. After releasing the sheet and halyard from the cockpit, I crawled along the deck on hands and knees, half kneeling, half lying down, as *Sea Sharp* flailed. I had to hang on, but I needed free hands. I couldn't take time to unsnap the sail from the headstay, so I stuffed it into its bag and tied it securely to the bow pulpit. That took nearly an hour in a pummeling storm. While I was up there, one wave washed over the boat, submerging the bow, filling my boots, and chilling my skin. Icy water ran down my neck and back.

Next, I hauled in the main sheet to ease the boom. I had to raise the weight of the boom with the topping lift, but I just couldn't muster the strength. I locked one arm around the backstay to keep myself standing. But I still couldn't raise that boom with only one free hand, so I lowered it over the cabin. I released the halyard, and the sail came down over the deck. What a mess! What a slipshod sailor I had become! I was fighting a dragon by the tail there, and it was about to smash me before devouring me, my boat, and all.

Without any sail, *Sea Sharp* was a cork at the ocean's mercy. She nearly lay on her side until the weight of water caught her keel and righted her. I stood on the cabin top, arms flung around the mast, clinging to this wild, bucking horse on water. As soon as I could, I worked my way back to the cockpit, exhausted and panting. The battle had drained me. I downed a food bar, glugged some luke-warm coffee, and felt my energy restored. After all that, the wind hadn't eased at all.

I lost track of time. Minutes blurred to hours; hours passed in oblivion. Meanwhile, my mind tussled with the tasks at hand: staying alive and keeping that boat afloat. We couldn't continue without sail; we needed stability and steerage. That meant I must go forward once again. But I couldn't open the cabin; I knew to keep it sealed as waves crashed over the top. One big wave coming aboard—and there were many—could flood the inside.

We all find hidden reserves of strength when the need arises. I crawled to the foredeck once again, pulling the storm trysail through the forward hatch. After fastening the trysail slides to the mast's track and attaching its halyard, I returned to the cockpit's protection to raise the sail. With that done, I trimmed the sheets and secured them. Now I could bring *Sea Sharp* back on course—and work on fixing me.

I have no idea where the time went. The day was gone, light fading fast, as I thanked the heavens for giving me the strength to secure the sails. I had done none of my usual chores, but I didn't care. *Sea Sharp* and I remained above water, and that's all that mattered.

Ritalin had become my "courage pills." I took one every three or four hours, washed down with spit. I needed them. The tempest wasn't done, and neither was I.

The storm's full fury hit before the following dawn. *Sea Sharp* was small and this was our first real trial, which made it all the worse. The wind blew forty miles per hour; the water submerged us several times. The first time it happened, I closed my eyes and held my breath. You know that saying about life flashing before the eyes, just before the end? Well, it's true. I saw the footage of my life during that storm.

Still, the seas went even higher. From the depths of the trenches, I looked up toward the next mountain of water, nearly as high as my mast. The boat's bow pointed up to the heavens one moment, then crested the wave and shot straight down. I gave up steering; *Sea Sharp* did better on her own, as though she could sense the waves and roll with them.

At one point I pumped the bilge ninety-two strokes; a normal amount was twelve to twenty strokes. We were filling up fast. Later, a wave lurched the boat and threw me against the coaming, stealing my wind. It hurt to cough or breathe, and I wondered if I had cracked a rib. I looked up at a wall of water and saw a log aimed straight at me like a torpedo. It shot in front of the bow, just inches away. I have no idea where it came from. A wrecked ship? The Alaskan coast? It could have knocked me down, clobbered my head, punctured the boat. It could have killed me six different ways, but it flew right by.

The cabin lamp ran out of kerosene one night. I didn't know which night; I was still confused about time, still battling the weather. So there was no friendly light from below, only darkness. The air was so filled with spray and foam, I couldn't tell where the ocean ended and air began. But there were small blessings. My wet clothes served as insulation, and I was never cold. I felt no hunger, so I didn't care that food was beyond my reach. And through that ride, circumstances could have spiraled far, far worse. I never grew sick. I never tipped over.

The hours passed, and I was numbed to a stupor. There was nothing more I could do, so I left it to God. I wondered whether combat troops felt the same when they were trapped in battle with no control over their fate. Even the most skillful soldiers sometimes die. So do sailors. I prayed the prayer of my childhood, the one about accepting what can't be changed, changing what can be, and having the wisdom to know the difference.

I think the lack of sleep, the drugs, and the dismay addled my brain. I heard noises. I saw visions in the tempest, distorted figures in the phosphorescent light, and the wind's high-pitched screaming in the sails. Was I losing my mind? The will to survive is one of humanity's strongest instincts, I can attest. Yet it occurred to me that I could step into the great abyss and leave this rage behind. It would be so easy to make the storm stop, just for me.

And then it all passed.

The whistling stopped; the winds slackened. What day was it? I had no idea. I couldn't remember sleeping, though I must have dozed at times. I ached everywhere. I crawled into the cabin, shed my clothes, zipped into the sleeping bag. And I slept—without a single thought of the boat before I dipped into sleep. But even sleep was trauma. I dreamed of *Sea Sharp* submerged, fish swimming past the cabin window. I felt the boat lying on her side.

But none of that was real.

When I finally awoke below, my skin was mottled black-and-blue and my ribs pained me with every move. But I was alive. The flesh sagged from my bones. I hadn't eaten a real meal in some time, a long time, longer than I could clearly recall. My diet of "courage pills" had taken its toll.

I found *Sea Sharp* in irons, dead in the water, with one sail backing the other. We were just bobbing in place. I wasn't concerned; it had happened before. I cinched my rib cage in an Ace bandage, bound as tight as could be. I cooked oatmeal, opened a can of tomato juice, and poured hot coffee. When I turned on the radio, I learned the date: Wednesday, June 30. The last day I had marked on the calendar was Tuesday, June 24. Five days gone, and I couldn't account for the time. Had the storm lasted three days? Had I slept two?

We had covered ninety-six miles in that storm, though they were not far forward. Instead, they were excruciating miles up, down, and every which way. I sat silently, thinking a prayer of thanks for the sunshine that day after so much darkness. I trimmed the trysail and reset our course; that was all I could muster in my exhaustion.

Food and rest were my two biggest needs. I ate again, chicken and dumplings, canned of course; and I managed to squirt gravy everywhere. I laughed out loud, a hearty and healthy laugh fully deserved and thoroughly needed. Then I cleaned up the mess and slept in peace.

FIVE

Whispers at Sea

A new month. I flipped the calendar to July, drank a Coke in celebration, and wondered again about the mystery man who wanted the bottles. I settled into the cockpit for an afternoon of writing. The weather had warmed, and I was comfortable in a single sweater after days of being all bundled in layers. I couldn't wait for the trade winds, when I could shed these constricting clothes. Modest whitecaps studded the waves, and a gooney bird landed nearby. I noticed it had only one leg, which immediately won my sympathy. I tossed it sliced bread and made myself another little friend.

Already, it had been half my estimated time at sea, yet I had covered just one-third the distance. It was time *Sea Sharp* underwent a thorough maintenance inspection. For days I had heard water sloshing somewhere but didn't know where. I searched on hands and belly and found the source by accident. A can had rolled beneath the compartment housing the head, and when I reached to grab it, my hand plunged deep into water. I moved everything out of the way, lifted the floorboards, and found water inundating the two forward bilge sections. Cup by cup, I bailed that water into buckets, ten in all. The bilge drains were clogged; it would be another half-day's job to fix them. Such is the banality behind the great sea adventures.

Every day I tried to celebrate something. July 3 marked three weeks on water, an admirable feat in my estimation. I took inventory of everything about me. Physically and mentally I rated a B, though at times I felt terminally low. *Sea Sharp* was doing fine: nothing broken, nothing lost. I had used only seven gallons of water, which left me enough for eight or nine more weeks—God forbid. I had hardly dented my canned-food supply. Looking back in time, the journey seemed to have progressed apace, but gazing forward, another three weeks seemed an eternity to me. I had 868 miles behind me; 1,500 lay ahead.

By Independence Day I had reached the trade winds, a fitting accomplishment for the holiday. *Sea Sharp* leapt to new motion patterns. Up, down, roll to one side; up, down, roll to the other. High waves, low waves, pointed waves, round waves, slanting waves, waves atop each other—this was all new to me. Like a switch flipped in the wind, we hit this air and everything changed. *Sea Sharp* maintained just enough speed to stay ahead of the breaking seas most of the time. Every seventh or eighth roll brought a granddaddy that would fill the cockpit and deliver me a bath. I didn't care. The air was warm and I sailed au naturel.

With winds now coming from astern, it was finally time to hoist the twin genoas and poles. What a sight she was. I could sail a steady course now, with only occasional minor adjustments.

The weather was different here, mercurial: wispy white clouds and attractive sky one minute, dismal squalls the next. I could see them coming, a black horizon headed my way, and I would gather salty clothes to hang on deck for a good, warm rinsing.

And I—I stood beneath the rain, reveling in a shower dumped from the sky.

Many hours, *Sea Sharp* and I rode the proverbial sea of enchantment. One day I sailed through a school of porpoises arcing around the boat. Flying fish were new companions, too, shooting from the water en masse, glittering like raindrops in the sun. At night they were drawn to the running lights, and by morning I had to clean little fish off the deck. My one-legged gooney often was there, too, for its daily visit.

I was intrigued by the Portuguese man-of-war, a jellyfish known as a "living sailboat." Its body, like an inflated bladder, has a fluted ridge that catches the wind like a sail. It moves in schools like miniscule boats, tacking across a bay. If necessary, they can deflate themselves and hide. Their defense is a set of long, stringy tentacles hanging from the body, which inflict painful stings. I discovered this by accident one day while scooping them into a bucket for a closer examination. A man-of-war is a beauty to admire from afar.

I acquired so many friends of the sea, but I wondered when I might meet another human. The Transpacific Yacht Race had started July 4, and I tried to calculate when and where our charts might cross. I listened to the news, but there were no happenings close by. There had been an earthquake in Alaska and a tidal wave heading for Honolulu. People fled the coast. Los Angeles mariners stood guard, ready to move out their boats. I knew I was safer here than I would have been on shore.

My weeks were gliding by. By July 8 I had averaged 3.6 knots, five days in a row. "My calculations and speed are still holding good. If it will only continue," I told my diary, "twelve and a half days more!" Anticipation grew, and I invented ways to occupy my mind. I rattled my brain with navigation possibilities and probabilities and with continual guesses at when I might arrive and in what manner. At steady speeds, I surmised, I would reach Waikiki by midnight on July 20.

I exercised routinely, sit-ups and bicycling steps, preparing again for the demands of land. I often stood watching the horizon, making my legs do all the balancing. I stepped up and down the only step on board: a meager eighteen inches into the cabin. If I failed these routines, my legs could lose so much muscle after all this time at sea that I wouldn't be able to walk on land.

Despite these mental and physical exercises, I still felt anxious, a bit bored. It was time. Finally, I reached for the book, the one and only book tucked in the back of the hanging locker. I plucked it from the shelf, only to find I had read it before: James Bond in *The Spy Who Loved Me*.

No matter, by the end of the voyage I would read it three more times.

By the end of the voyage, I had also mastered the art of self-steering with the twin gennys, making *Sea Sharp* guide our way. I was spending most of my time in the cabin. Except to check the boat and perform daily chores, I saw no reason to expose myself to extra sun and wind. I devised a rocking chair for added comfort. I blew up the air mattress halfway, folded one-third of it under for the seat, and used the other two-thirds as a head and backrest, placed crosswise between the bunks. My bony body was suitably padded against the swelling ocean, allowing my many bruises and calluses to heal. I spent hours this way.

One night, the radio burbled news of Hawaii. "You are listening to KGMB Honolulu."

It was a garbled reception, but what a joy to hear it! I calculated only 240 hours and 875 miles to go. From then on I scanned the horizon every hour for masts and sails, hoping to spot a Transpac racing boat, despite the odds. *Sea Sharp*, so small, would disappear in the troughs of the ocean when viewed from a larger boat far away. But still, I hoped and gazed.

Then, one day I heard race results on air. The *Ticonderoga*, a seventy-two-foot ketch, led the race just six hundred miles offshore. I calculated her speed and position and figured she averaged 250 miles a day—a significant leap from our average of 83.9 miles a day since reaching the trades. I cheered for *Ticonderoga* as she crossed the finish line that night, with her red and white spinnaker flying. It was a record-setting win of nine days, thirteen hours, fifty-one minutes, and two seconds.

I began to think again, about returning to life on land. How would it feel to turn on a faucet? Flush a toilet? Walk from room to room? It had been so long that I feared I had forgotten the rhythm of ordinary actions. Would a ringing phone sound familiar? Freeway horns honking? Human voices? I could remember minute details of all my friends' faces, but I couldn't recall the tones of their voices.

I thought about business and pesky little tasks. I reminded myself to call my insurance company. I couldn't afford to insure *Sea Sharp* while sailing, so I would have to renew the policy on land. I tried to remember my car. How did it feel to turn the key and drive? I tried to picture my wardrobe. So much effort we spend on appearance, and yet I could barely remember the contents of my closet.

I hauled out my departure outfit from the hanging locker and thought of when I would be wearing it again, when I'd turn it into an arrival suit. My purse was there inside the locker, and suddenly I remembered money. I had never before gone thirty days without spending a penny; how strange to count the coins. Four dollars and thirty-two cents, that was all the loot aboard. That would not be much if we were ever to meet pirates.

I wrote letters to my closest friends, thanking them for their friendship, saying the things we so often don't. And I wrote lists of all that had to be done. I would have to retrieve the dock lines, sail covers, and fender. Where had I stored them? I wanted *Sea*

Sharp to sparkle for our arrival, and I hoped the same of myself. I painted my toenails a cheery pink but waited to do the fingernails until we got closer to shore. My hands, like sandpaper, showed the weathering of time at sea. They were scaling and peeling as though diseased. A hot shower and shampoo topped my list of "wants" for when we hit land.

For hours, I watched the sea and wondered what I would find in Hawaii. Did anyone know I was coming? For me, it was a countdown with 185 hours remaining. Seven more times to pump the bilge, clean the running lights, and go to sleep. Hugh had challenged me to sight land within two hours of the time that I calculated I would. By the time I started my count down, I had refigured my land sighting to be 9:00 a.m. on July 20.

After all these days on water, I had seen nature through the seafarer's eyes. I had seen both her glory and her fury. The air out there was so clean and pure; the sunshine so dramatic in the way it converged with the abysmal depths of sea. I grew acutely aware of change in light and color—from dark to bright, pastels and half tones, and brilliance and saturation.

At night I would peer over the side into the pools of flashing phosphorescence. Sometimes I saw pairs of green shining eyes—the fish I knew by day or a monster down under? Other times, we sailed through acres of plankton, and the black waters would gleam with millions of miniscule lights. Such magnificence, such turbulence. So much at nature's mercy.

One night, I awoke in a startle. I heard a soft, soothing voice calling my name. "Sharon, Sharon," it sang. I darted upright, flung open the hatch, and looked around. Nothing, of course—but that voice sounded so real to me. "Sharon, Sharon."

The solitary mind is a master of imagination.

SIX

A Life to Ponder

I made peace with myself slowly in that boat, in the doldrums and in the frightening grip of the storm. The sea affords enough space and time for thinking fully, and I spent lonely hours mired in my own messy past. If I could do it all again, I wondered, would I have had children? If I hadn't had any children, I couldn't have left them.

I was born in a railroad-line shack in Battleground, Washington, on May 29, 1930. My parents named me Phyllis Mae. My father had worked as a dump-truck driver, but he lost his job in the Great Depression before I was born. So he took the family to live on his sister's farm in eastern Oregon, where he sharecropped and herded sheep.

When I was seventeen months old, my mother's youngest sister died back in Battleground, so she took us with her to the funeral. It was a bitterly cold day in December, and not long after, my mother developed pneumonia. She died in the following January of 1932. My elder sister, Elizabeth, and I got shuffled from one family to the next until finally our father gave us away to a couple named Ted and Alma. They adopted us and took us to live in Milton-Freewater, a little speck of a town in the Blue Mountains of northeastern Oregon. And with that, we were given new lives, new identities. My sister was renamed Mariel, and I became Sharon.

When I was nine, my adoptive family moved south to Prineville, in Oregon's desert plains. It was high and dry country flush with cattle and timber. I never got close to the sea, nothing more than the rivers and lakes that dot the Oregon countryside. I didn't see the ocean until I was seventeen, standing on a cliff at the Oregon coast. It was big and it was mighty. That was all I thought of the sea at that time. I don't remember being impressed.

In school, I was a straight-A student. I loved going to school, but I hated going home. From the age of twelve, I did the family chores, cooking and cleaning and laundering. My adoptive mother always declared, "I just don't feel well today," and so a grown woman's chores were given to a child.

I sang in the church choir and played the cello for sixteen years. I played several different instruments in the school band. It was wartime in the spring of my junior year, and the band director was drafted. He left, and I finished the term as band leader for ball games and school events.

Ted and Alma never got along very well. He was a nice guy, but she was cranky and clashed with the rest of us. When I think back on those years, I hear the screaming, the nagging, the repetitious insults coming from Alma in the bedroom. I learned to be two people, two Sharons: one Sharon at home, another Sharon away from her. I learned never to be disrespectful or tell a lie. I only answered what she asked, but I didn't always tell the entire story. She used to belittle me, to needle me with disparagement. How she used to doubt me! "I don't know how anyone likes you. I don't see how you have any friends," she would say. What Alma never understood was that my friends didn't want to come around when she was there. No one wanted to experience the wrath of Alma.

I remember one morning when Ted was preparing for work and she kept ranting. I turned to him and said, "Why don't you leave that woman?" He said nothing. He just looked at me with the sorry eyes of a puppy dog. That house would never change.

Ted was a watchmaker with a small jewelry store. As a teenager, he had suffered a hunting accident and lost a leg. Wearing an artificial limb, he could never do the things with me that he might have, but I always knew he was proud of my accomplishments. I always felt a little pity for the man.

But I loved my childhood in the outdoors, and I grew up like a tomboy—hunting and fishing, camping and swimming. I raised rabbits, keeping a few as pets and butchering the others for meat. I fly-fished from the banks of the Crooked River. I hiked through the desert, searching for arrowheads and pretty rocks. I did anything I could to stay outside.

I loved to hunt. When I was in high school, I wrote a term paper on birds and collected a feather from every specimen in my report: a crow, a blackbird, a hawk, a pheasant, a duck, and a magpie. I had to shoot them, of course, to complete the project. I even knocked the tail feather off a wild canary with a .22, catching my specimen but sparing the bird. Being a tomboy never bothered me. I was the first girl in Crook County High history to graduate with a credit in mechanical drawing, which I took instead of home economics. I figured I had already played the role of maid and housekeeper, so there was no need for further study in that realm.

I never thought much about the possibilities of life beyond school. I never knew I could have worked my way through college; I had never had a job outside the home, a job that paid money. So when graduation time came around, I did the first thing I could think of to get myself out of the house and onto my own track: I married my sister's brother-in-law, Don. With a high school diploma barely six weeks old, I became a missus. I knew nothing then, nothing about life, nothing beyond our insular little town of 2,500 people.

My wedding doesn't stick in my memory. I don't recall what it was like. I remember more of my sister Mariel's—she had made her bridesmaids' dresses, red taffeta with white satin trim and long ribbons down the back. I wore Mariel's gown for my own wedding and topped it with a long veil. Don and I were married in a church on a hundred-degree day, which made for a sauna of the outdoor reception; that much I remember. Alma and I fought that day; I remember that, too—something about the cake. She went inside and seethed and fumed as she often did.

Two weeks later when Don and I returned to the house to get my things, it happened again. Alma exploded, and Don told her never to berate me that way again. She raged, madder than ever, and told us to get out, to never come back. So we did, and I didn't.

Don and I moved first to The Dalles on the Columbia River where he had a small cherry orchard; we later moved to Walla Walla, Washington, where he enrolled in Whitman College. When we first married, I didn't know about keeping house or paying bills. Cooking and cleaning, yes. Finances, no. Growing up, I did all the shopping, but I had no idea what it cost. It was all charged to Ted and Alma's account, and I never saw the bills. So when I first went shopping for Don, I bought spices and flour and everything to stock a kitchen. The bill came to something like $50, which was a lot for us back then, and I went home and cried and cried. I couldn't believe I had spent so much, more than I thought we could afford. It was my first inkling that I might be a mismatch for the life I'd made.

I knew nothing about having babies either, but that was what Don wanted more than anything. I don't remember ever thinking about having children. I guess I assumed everybody did. But nobody ever told me about labor pains or what to do with a baby or how to feed him, bathe him, raise him. I mean, I knew nothing.

It took twenty-two hours of labor to bring Sandy, our first-born, into this world. Don was in the waiting room, wondering what was taking so long. The doctor used forceps because I'm so small boned. I had been given a spinal, and when I got home, I couldn't get my head off the pillow. It was awful. I had no sense of motherhood. I had an aunt in Seattle who came to help with the baby. She even made my formula. We lived in a basement apartment. Though it was August and hot outside, my aunt turned on the oven to heat up the kitchen because it was still cool within. She wanted to give the baby a warm bath. I'd washed Sandy before, and she'd turned blue because she had grown so cold. I just didn't know; I didn't think.

Three years later we had a son, Dennis. I stayed home to care for the children and keep house, and so I was smack back in the middle of domesticity, the life I had so desperately wanted to leave. The days began with ennui and ended with downright depression.

Don did take good care of us—that much I can't deny. I never had money to call my own, but he gave me whatever I needed. Don was good to me, a considerate husband. And I didn't want it.

We didn't even bicker, but we probably would have reached that point. There wasn't anything wrong except me. Don wasn't unhappy: the house was clean, his dinner was fixed, and the children were cared for. They were his children; they weren't mine. Come five o'clock, little Sandy was at the door waiting for him to come home. I was the caretaker, Don was the daddy, and the children knew it instinctively. He'd get up in the night with them; they didn't come to me. Don tended their coughs and colds, their tears and fears.

Housewives back then didn't just quit to pursue self-fulfillment; women didn't make those calls. In today's world, it would be different. Yet I felt empty, as though I were looking for something. For years, we never took a vacation. I felt there had to be more for me than cooking and cleaning and raising children.

I took a break. I went to Vegas. I booked a room at the El Rancho and spent five days. It was the first casino hotel on the Las Vegas Strip, the one place that would make Las Vegas famous. There was nothing before El Rancho and almost nothing around. There was just wide open desert, ages and ages between the airport and town. The El Rancho is gone now, burned to the ground decades ago in a fire. But back then, the El Rancho was the Vegas that everyone dreamed Vegas would be.

I didn't talk to anyone; I just ate and thought and watched the people. I put on fancy clothes, and I wandered around the craps tables. I remember the way people dressed, the way they walked and talked. They strutted their money. That was my first trip out of the Northwest, my first exposure to anything but the life I'd known. The El Rancho took me away to a place in my mind I'd never been allowed to visit.

That trip was the beginning of the end for my marriage. I returned to Oregon and thought I might make it, if I could just get away every now and then—but of course I couldn't. I just couldn't do it. It wasn't long before Don and I talked. I told him I'd stay another year if he wanted, but then I'd be gone.

"No," he insisted. "If you're going, go now."

So I did. I took the car, my cello, my clothes, $50, and a few misgivings that wouldn't let go. I stayed away for a few weeks, but a nagging guilt overcame me. I even thought of suicide. OK, I thought, I'll try once more. I'll go home.

I returned, but nothing really changed. I didn't feel any better. Don didn't plead with me to stay. He just sadly let me go.

That time, I left for good. Sandy was four and Dennis was less than a year. I didn't see my children for another eight or nine years; Don and I thought it would be best. I wrote to them. I sent them presents for birthdays and Christmas, but it got so hard because I never heard back. Never got a thank-you card, just an occasional letter from Don with a few snapshots and an update on the kids' progress in school.

Once I bought Sandy a bicycle, and I drove four hundred miles to deliver it in person. But no one was home when I arrived, and another bicycle sat by the door. So I left. I could never again fill the shoes I'd already taken off and packed away.

When Don and I divorced, Mariel's husband forbade her to see me. It was his brother, after all, whom I had forsaken. But Mariel and I had been close in those days, and she snuck out of her house to meet me. We had an hour at an obscure highway restaurant. She wanted answers from me, wanted to know what had compelled me to leave. I told her it was all about me and this insufferable sense of nothingness I felt inside.

And that was it; no more contact with Mariel. She, too, vanished from my life.

Looking back is hindsight, utterly inconsequential; but I would have done it all differently if I had the chance. If I had only known, I would have gone to college. That's what I wanted to do, but I didn't know it. I didn't know how. Back then, guidance counselors didn't exist in small-town American high schools. No one spoke to me about higher education until graduation day, and by that point I was already spoken for. I had made a commitment, and I didn't break it. But I should have.

That's my life mistake. Who knows where I'd be, who I'd be, if I had ended my marriage before it began. I could have been anyone, or no one. I probably wouldn't have made my way to Los Angeles, to my second husband, Chuck. Or to the job I held for twelve years in a dentist's office. Or to widowhood, which came much too soon.

And I probably wouldn't have been on that boat in the middle of the Pacific.

SEVEN

A One-Hand Finish

The buzz began on land, the sailing world priming for my return, but I didn't know. I cruised through my solitary universe, wondering whether any landlubbers remembered me.

But people remembered. The navy pilot who had circled my boat and tipped his wings reported the sighting, and it made radio news. The pilot said he couldn't believe the view of *Sea Sharp* bobbing around that great ocean expanse, like a toy in eternity. He had taken pictures from the plane and sent enlargements to Al. But I didn't know.

I didn't know any of that, nor did I know of the downpour that followed—a flood of phone calls, strangers calling Al in the night, wondering whether he had heard from me. He was inundated with questions. He reminded the callers I was in the middle of the Pacific on a boat with a one-way radio. No, he hadn't heard a thing. No one had.

Al closed his school for a while and headed to Hawaii early. When he reached Honolulu, he informed a coast guard captain of my impending arrival. The man asked for a complete description of the boat, a list of all equipment and gear aboard, the quantity of food and water with which I'd embarked. Turns out, this captain was the same coast guard captain who had warned me against my voyage before it began. When he learned of all the preparation I'd put into this journey, he apologized. He had judged me before knowing the facts. He had read my letter to the Southern California Yachting Association and told the crowd I was a "kook," who would cost taxpayers thousands of dollars for my search and rescue. But he changed his mind and acknowledged his underestimation of my chutzpah.

My friends—Dione, Sandy, Barbara, and their children—had planned a Hawaiian vacation, July 12–22, hoping to greet me. Those dates, a window and a deadline, nagged at me. I had to get back, I kept thinking, though I knew nothing of the clamor on land. I just knew I had the date of a lifetime penciled on my calendar.

My friends would go to the Diamond Head and Koko Head lookout points, great volcanic promontories overlooking the ocean near Honolulu. They would scan the channel, watching for signs of me. I was to fire a flare when I neared Waikiki. I was not to sail through the breaking surf alone, too dangerous. The gang took turns at their lookouts, day and night. They left only for food and regular phone calls to the coast guard to see whether anyone had reported news of *Sea Sharp*. They had a rented boat ready to meet me at the entrance buoy and bring me in. Even tourists volunteered to take a watch for a few hours at a time.

And I knew nothing of it. I worried that others would worry about me. I had estimated that my crossing would take thirty-five to forty days. Even with my slow start and light wind, I knew I would make it, but no one on land knew that and it troubled me. I had spotted several low-flying airplanes making their descents toward land—comforting sights to me. I must be getting closer, I thought. I added new foil to the radar reflector, to make it shine more brightly, just in case a pilot up there were to notice my little craft below.

The Hawaiian radio stations were starting to come in clearly on my radio, so I listened to a baseball game one afternoon. Between innings, the announcers discussed the two boats remaining in the Transpac race. And then I heard my name. "What about that woman?" one announcer asked the other. "She's still out there, too."

The words threw me in a fit of delight. Such a small thing to squelch my fears. It was the first reference to me and *Sea Sharp* I had heard in weeks—small proof that we still drifted through people's minds.

As of Monday, July 19, we were getting close, so close I thought I could smell land on the air. It would be a busy day. I took my last noon sight: thirty-six hours and 126 miles remaining. If all my calculations held true, I would spot land within twenty-one hours.

I was determined to make *Sea Sharp* spiffy. I wanted her looking like she was coming in from a Sunday sail, no worse for the wear, no signs of the five weeks she had endured on open seas. She needed work—her varnish lacked luster, her sides looked weathered, and she had suffered the corrosive traumas of salt. So I took cleaner and brush, and I scrubbed her up and down, just in time for a fortuitous shower that rinsed us both clean.

Sea Sharp was ready; it was time for me. I bathed in salt water, working my hair into a lather, a deep-down shampoo. Then I indulged: I dumped a gallon of precious fresh water over head and body. I used the same water to rinse my lingerie, then again to wipe finger marks from the cabin interior. I had fifteen gallons of water left, and I was sure I wouldn't need it.

My fingernails were long after seven weeks with no trim. I polished them twice, two careful coats applied between rolls of the ocean.

I listened to the radio again, and again I heard my name.

"Rugged but feminine" that's what Al called me. "I expect her tomorrow or the next day. Let's give her a chance to get here." He said it and I heard it 110 miles away from one another.

I sat down to my diary. "After twenty-four hundred logged miles, I feel I'm doing pretty well." I noted my last duties at sea—filling the lamps, fixing dinner, making my last night's bed. "By tomorrow night I'll have to be sailing this boat, even if it takes all night." At least, I thought it would be so. I was certain, wasn't I? But still, what if? "I know I'm right," I wrote to myself, "but . . . I'm strung up tighter than five banjo strings." How could a person be so sure yet so clueless? So full of faith yet so dubious? So certain of math and physics yet so skeptical of scientific truth? That is the beautiful, scary dichotomy of sailing psychology.

Suddenly I realized I needed clothes, which I hadn't worn in days. I'd have to prepare my going-ashore attire. I didn't want anyone to spot me in the buff—how embarrassing that would be! Especially if I got really excited and jumped up, waving to the crowds.

That night, I fell to sleep quickly but awoke four times to check the compass, anxious for the coming day. At 5:40 a.m. I was wide awake but wouldn't let myself look outside. It would be three more hours at least before land would appear on the horizon. Waiting, waiting, I returned to sleep.

On July 20 I awoke for good at 8:30 in the morning, opened the hatch, and greeted fresh air. There it was: LAND! A spectacular sight, if still only a smudge in the distance. A colossal cloudbank off the port bow obscured the outline, but I could feel its presence. It was there. Land. And birds flying everywhere.

Oh, where was my camera? I'd imagined this picture a thousand times, but nothing in my mind rivaled the beauty in reality. The sky, the water, both were deep blue; the clouds were never fluffier; the whitecaps, never whiter; the birds, never soaring so gracefully about me. I kissed *Sea Sharp*. My whole body tingled. I had just a moment of sadness for the memory of Sarah Beth-Ann, who should have been there too. Then, I felt nothing but joy.

The chart told me I'd found the island of Molokai, but I couldn't be certain until the cloud cover lifted and I could identify the island by sight. But what a euphoric guess.

Coffee never tasted so good as it did that morning, and I filled the thermos so I wouldn't have to light the Sterno again. I could live on candy, crackers, and nuts from there on. I dressed in old clothes, appropriate for the spray; my arrival outfit, packed in stowage since the day I departed, would wait for later. *Sea Sharp* sailed on ideal seas that morning, leaving a necklace of foam in her diminishing wake.

By 5:30 p.m. I could discern a speck of land beneath thick clouds off the starboard bow. I knew it was Oahu. As the sun set behind the island, I photographed a welcome silhouette. Soon, the navigation lights would come on at Makapuu and Diamond Head, and I would be able to fix my bearings and set our final course. Only twenty miles to go. The seas hadn't changed, and the wind remained calm all through the Molokai channel. I said another prayer, "Bless you, Lord, for delivering *Sea Sharp* and me safely. And thank you, the wind is just fine."

Hugh, my navigation master, had been right after all. The island was precisely where my chart had said it would be.

My eyes were fixed on that land, hoping my friends would spot me coming through. But that would not happen. As fate would have it, my friends had left for dinner at 8:30 and returned two hours later, while I slipped by unnoticed in the interim.

When I rounded Diamond Head, Waikiki beamed like a torch. All those lights—such a glittering array—ran inland, fanning up the hillsides and igniting the island in color. The city looked dressed for a holiday, though it was an ordinary night to everyone but me.

Just another hour before I would approach the buoy that would signal journey's end. Back on July 13 I had calculated time and mileage in my diary, and I had estimated an arrival on July 21 at 2:00 a.m. It looked like I'd be within hours, perhaps minutes, of my calculations. I had hoped for a daylight arrival, but so be it.

A nighttime approach meant three things: I must stay well away from shore, avoiding the jagged coastline and reefs near the harbor entrance. I must fire a flare gun, and if no one were to see it, I must tack back and forth until sunrise. Finally, I must sail to the lee of the island if I found myself in trouble, and wait so the trade winds wouldn't swallow me up and sweep me out to Samoa.

The time came.

I luffed my sails to let *Sea Sharp* rise and fall with the swells. I retrieved my flare gun and cartridge from the life raft; loaded the cartridge; and with my arm outstretched, pointed the pistol to the wind, just as I'd learned in sailing class a few months back. Bracing for the recoil, I squeezed the trigger.

Nothing happened.

Just as I brought my arm down closer to my body for better leverage, that's when it fired. The gun flew out of my hand and struck my right shoulder. I heard the gun ricochet off the boat; I thought it had flown over the side. I fell backward, stunned and blinded. The flare had shot too low for the parachute to open; no one would see it. No one would know I was there.

I picked myself up from the cockpit and sat in a stupor, regaining my sight. The empty flare cartridge lay beside my feet. I reached to retrieve it, but my hand wouldn't work. Panicked, I tried to move the fingers of my injured right hand but felt nothing.

Nothing.

The hand simply didn't move, wouldn't do what my brain told it to. When the gun flew from my hand, it had bent my thumb backward against my arm. Now my hand and wrist had frozen, numb. My shoulder ached, and so did the elbow I hit in the fall. All those people on Waikiki were in sight, within reach, just a mile between me and shore. But I didn't know how to get there. They didn't know I had arrived. So the distance between us meant nothing. I might as well have been in the dead of the ocean again.

As my hand slowly regained sensation, it swelled bigger and bigger, up to my elbow. Blinding pain shot up my arm. I must have broken my wrist; I knew it. I wrapped my hand and forearm in an Ace bandage, flung open the first-aid kit, and swallowed two codeine pills, ignoring the warning not to take more than one pill every four hours. I was in pain and I needed it to stop. I had no time for lectures.

What next? I couldn't sit until morning—I would be carried to shore. And what an awful ending that would be: *Sea Sharp* breaking apart on a reef. The twin poles and genoas were still raised, so I couldn't tack. With only one functional hand, I couldn't change sails. I had no choice but to maneuver toward the island's lee side, Arrival Plan C. I remember thinking at the time, "What could possibly go wrong if I'd already made it that far?"

I trimmed sails as best I could so we'd move slowly. Suddenly, *Sea Sharp* lit up like a bonfire. Crossing our bow was a tugboat towing two barges, shining a blinding spotlight first on us and then on the barges, so we wouldn't sail over their towlines. I shined my spotlight on our sails so they were sure to see us, blinked sos ten times, and sighed with relief—surely they would help. They would report my message, and soon someone would rescue me.

But the night went on and on, and no one came.

By dawn we had rounded the island, and I felt a fluky breeze on the lee side. Hardly a ripple marked the water. I was drifting then, on a desultory sea. I was safe from the clutch of the trade winds, but I was nowhere near a safe harbor. I downed more codeine, trying hard to ignore the pain, which had not subsided. My arm had swollen to twice its size.

I listened to the radio. At least I was being talked about.

"Any word of *Sea Sharp* or Sharon Sites?" the announcer asked.

"No, nothing," the coast guard official replied.

I listened and sobbed. ·

At last I forced myself to face the emerging day. I had one remaining tactic, one last trick in my bag. I took a distress flag and dye marker from the life raft and, with teeth and one hand, raised the flag on the halyard to the starboard spreader. Using my one good hand and feet to hold the can, I pried the dye marker open with a screwdriver. The dye sprinkled on the water, spreading and growing, painting almost an acre of water in brilliant silver. Surely someone—*someone*—would see that.

In the following two hours, I watched as first an airliner and then three military planes flew overhead. But nobody paid attention to my glittering stain. The flare gun, I found, had not fallen overboard after all. It was lodged between the coaming and the life raft, which meant I still had one more option: I could try the gun again.

As I weighed that option, an engine droned; a powerboat was cresting the horizon. What a glorious sound! But the boat motored close to shore, and it probably wouldn't come near enough for me to flag it down. That pistol was my only recourse.

That time, I used a smaller flare without a parachute in an effort to minimize damage. It took a long time to rustle up the courage as I held that gun in the air with my one good hand, bracing myself for the impact. I held my breath and squeezed. The flare worked, arched high into the air, and I thanked the Lord. The powerboat quickly changed its course and headed toward me. They had seen my flare. I quivered in the knees, weak with pain and relief.

"Are you in trouble?" the skipper asked. Those were the first four words I'd heard from another human being in thirty-eight days. It was a charter fishing boat, the *Catherine S*, with several passengers aboard.

I tried to speak. I wasn't sure a sound would come out, but a feeble "Yes" managed to escape. "Have you heard of the woman sailing from California?"

He had.

"That's me. I'm Sharon Sites."

He thought it was a joke until I showed them *Sea Sharp*'s nameplate and I pointed around the boat and I kept insisting. Finally, the *Catherine S* passengers believed.

What had I done to my wrist? Everyone was curious and concerned. "I'm too embarrassed to tell you," I said, so ashamed of my mishap. But I told the skipper I couldn't use my hand. Did he have a radio? Would he please call the coast guard and ask if they would notify Al and my friends so they could come and get me? Would he please tell the world on land that I was there, that I was alive?

The skipper repeated my message then made the call. The coast guard would send a cutter for me—not exactly my vision of a grand reentrance, but I was in no position to protest. The *Catherine S* would stand by as I waited for help.

"We planned a day of marlin fishing," the skipper said. "What a surprise to catch you instead."

I must have looked awful, and one of the women aboard asked whether I wanted help cleaning up. But no one else had touched *Sea Sharp* since I left, and I was determined to finish the journey without anyone else's footsteps aboard that boat. I explained and politely declined her offer.

Instead, I gussied up myself as best I could. I went below deck to prepare, to change into pretty white clothes that had been stowed, it seemed, an eternity. Seven weeks since I last applied makeup, but it was time. *No matter what, I will come in looking like a lady.* That was my vow, a promise I had made to myself before leaving. And I would. I refused to come out looking like a derelict; the same for *Sea Sharp* as well. We both needed to look our best. But our best wasn't very good with only my left hand.

When I popped my head through the hatch again, I felt like

a changed woman. And I couldn't believe the sight: boats every-where, boats motoring toward me, boats circling, boats bobbing around us. Since the skipper had called the coast guard, word was out; and here came boats of every size—a destroyer, even. On the radio, programs were interrupted with announcements of our sighting. I thought I was hallucinating. The codeine had left me foggy, eight pills in ten hours. Was it real?

The coast guard cutter drew near, and my fellow passengers aboard the *Catherine S* bade farewell. "We'll be on our way now. Good luck!" And off they went.

The cutter kept a distance. So big was it, so small were we. "Do you want me to put a man aboard to help you?" the captain shout-ed through a megaphone.

"No thank you," I answered. That was not what I wanted after all those solitary days. No way. They threw me a towline with a bowline knot already formed at the end. I brought it in through the bow pulpit and hung it over the bitt on the foredeck.

"Remember we're little and can't go very fast!" I yelled to the captain, my voice growing stronger, pumped on adrenaline. The faster a boat moves through water, the more friction on the hull. Speed can create enough suction to draw a boat underwater, and I had frantic visions of being hauled at twelve knots, which would surely submerge us. But that didn't happen. The captain smiled and pulled ahead slowly until the towline drew taut. And so began the very last leg of our journey.

I had to apologize to *Sea Sharp*; in my excitement and doped-up state, I hadn't thought about her. I could not stow her sails, and be-ing towed as we were, she did not reach land in the valiant manner I had imagined. *Sea Sharp* didn't look like the lady I knew she was.

But she followed loyally behind the cutter and didn't need me at the tiller. As we picked up speed, the ride grew wetter and rougher and my little boat tossed waves off her bow. I went below to avoid the spray, tuning in to the radio again.

"Yes, we can see it now. We're getting closer to her, ladies and gentlemen, it looks like a mighty little boat to us. It's really taking a rough ride, but we don't see any sign of the skipper on board. We're only about one hundred yards away now."

The man spoke of me! I stood up, poking my head and shoulders out of the hatch.

"There she is now! I can see her; she's waving to us. We can see a large bandage on her arm. Other than that, she's smiling and appears to be OK. She's truly a blonde, dressed in white slacks with a blue and white top."

Just as I had suspected, appearances mattered.

The blow-by-blow came from an eighty-foot press boat, decked with CBS cameras and cameramen, all poised to get the shot. I could see them, not so far away. They pulled alongside and copied our speed, hurling questions over water, boat to boat. What's the first thing I told them? The first words I offered?

"Never again!"

Never again would I attempt such an outlandish feat—I'm on record with that declaration, which appeared in a two-inch red headline in the *Honolulu Star-Bulletin*.

As we neared the harbor, my friends came alongside. We talked against the wind, all of us, friends and spectators asking questions: "How do you feel?" "Did you have trouble?" "How's the boat?" "Anything broken?" Then a Piper Cub flew overhead and dropped a message—an invitation to be the distinguished guest of the Royal Hawaiian Hotel, which would host a grand celebration for me.

And then silence. I just stared at the faces, overwhelmed, like a scene in a movie when the background noise fades to the quiet thoughts of a character's head.

Hundreds of people waited in the harbor and on the dock, but I had a hard time getting there. I couldn't stand alone on land. I hadn't eaten. I was groggy and drugged, and my legs didn't work when we finally disembarked the boat. Al picked me up and set me on the dock as the crowd grabbed me to prevent me from falling. I was guided all the way. Ten steps forward, I was covered in leis up to my chin. Hugs and smooches, a swarm of warmth. I wobbled through the chaos, such noise, such a cacophony of voices. Cheering and stomping, clapping, jostling. The scent of human beings—a smell I hadn't experienced in weeks. It was invigorating and intoxicating, but I felt claustrophobic. I felt woozy.

One little girl wrapped a handmade lei of dried seeds around my neck. She had asked for my safety in her bedtime prayers, her mother told me.

Another lady reached out to me. "I just want to touch you," she said. "You have done so much for womanhood."

Really? I thought, I wondered.

A well-dressed man at the end of the dock held a lei of red carnations. He was a manger of the Royal Hawaiian Hotel, the "Pink Palace of the Pacific," and he came with instructions to offer me anything I wanted, even a car.

I can't remember all the questions I was asked, or who asked them, or how I answered. It all felt like a dream. I remember thanking my friends and praising the Lord. I remember attributing my success to forces beyond my control. And I recall remarking, "A single-handed sail is one thing, but a one-handed sail is impossible."

I bowed out of the excitement and went to the hospital for an X-ray. My wrist was not broken after all, but I had a bad sprain and torn ligaments. Soak it regularly in hot water, keep it in a sling, and continue the codeine, the doctor told me, but no more than one pill every six hours. I gulped. I didn't confess the ten I had already swallowed.

I had a booking at the Waikikian Hotel, which put me in a penthouse suite. Who could forget the Waikikian? With its legendary lobby shaped like a giant hyperbolic paraboloid, an extraordinary three-dimensional shape like a saddle, with edges that seemed to rise toward the heavens.

When I opened the door, the room bloomed with bouquets, dozens, everywhere. I remember that room like my first boat. My room came with a baby grand piano, a kitchenette with bar, piped music, plush furniture, and a balcony the length of the room with views of Waikiki. A king-sized bed in the master bedroom was covered in orchid petals. The dressing room had a full wall of mirrors and a marble table. There was a telephone in every room; there was a telephone near the toilet. The faucets were roses carved of gold. Oh, what luxury! I had never seen anything like it before. It was a long way from Milton-Freewater, Oregon.

"Stay as long as you like," the hotel president told me. "Welcome to Hawaii."

It was marvelous, though I still couldn't walk alone, knees buckling with every attempt. But it didn't matter. So many people surrounded me, hour after hour, that I was never alone to actually have to stand on my two tremulous feet.

I had relished the thought of a hot shower and shampoo. The room spun and rolled as though I were back on the boat. I felt sick. With help from friends, I brushed my teeth, fixed my hair, and dressed for my party. I could have done none of it alone.

The Royal Hawaiian put on a grand gala that evening. A table was set in the main dining room, and an orchestra played traditional island music near the dance floor. I thought ravenously of food. I hadn't eaten since the previous morning, and I hadn't eaten land grub in thirty-nine days. I wanted everything I couldn't have on board: a salad with crisp lettuce, a tall glass of lemonade, a bowl of hot soup. Nothing extravagant, just enough to satisfy the strange cravings that pester the mind and belly after weeks of abstention. My wishes and more were served that night—prime rib and bright tropical fruits and ice cream sherbet.

Back in my suite that evening, calls and cables came from all over the world, and my friends took turns answering phones. We couldn't juggle all the calls. I talked and ate, talked and dressed, talked and bathed. Newspapers everywhere announced my feat. Like giddy schoolgirls on a sleepover, my friends and I stayed awake through the night, scanning the papers.

At 3:00 a.m. fatigue filtered through my body. I lay down, stretching across the mattress. My bed was big and soft, it wasn't rolling, I had plenty of room, and all was quiet. But I couldn't sleep. Nothing would put my mind to rest.

The next afternoon, I faced my first official press conference, which had been arranged so I could deliver the letter from Mayor Yorty of Los Angeles. The Honolulu mayor presented me with a bowl carved from monkeypod wood, a trophy commemorating my accomplishment.

I couldn't keep track of all the newspaper and magazine articles on my own, so I hired a clipping service to gather the stories about our journey. Those stories filled a scrapbook that would carry me through the years. The attention was flattering, of course, but I've always been boggled by the disparate interpretations of a single event. There were people who didn't accept my accomplishment, didn't believe I actually had done it alone. Some thought I had cheated, had masterminded a grand international deception. Rumor had it a Russian submarine had towed me over.

One California paper called me irresponsible. The cost of search-and-rescue operations would burden taxpayers for years to come as more people would try to replicate my feat and fail. Since a thirty-five-year-old widow had successfully sailed a small sailboat single-handedly to Honolulu, surely an armada of one-man or one-woman boats would follow in her wake, the paper wrote. While "the lady-sailor" succeeded, the paper warned, not all to follow would be so fortunate.

A Honolulu paper quoted a prominent boater who called my voyage a silly stunt. He reiterated the taxpayers' burden. "As a yachtsman, I am very displeased with the publicity she has latched onto." And a New Orleans paper concluded, "If she repeats this foolishness, eventually she'll make some man a good widower."

But praise outweighed the sniggering.

"Anyone who supposes that modern women have grown spoiled and weak-willed should consider the exploit of Sharon Sites," one Chicago editor wrote. He thought I had triumphed in a "woman-against-the-elements saga worthy of a book by Hemingway." And he thought my stick-to-itiveness demonstrated that "nothing, but nothing, can stop an American woman once her mind is made up."

From Oakland, California came, "Bully for Sharon Sites." I had made up my mind that I was going to do something, and I did it.

"Sharon Sites now takes her place as one of those humans who dared and won," a Pennsylvania paper wrote. My example might lend courage to others who usually would "settle for the humdrum and second best."

Stacks of mail arrived at the hotel—congratulatory cards, yacht club membership offers, party invitations, speaking requests, inquiries for pictures and autographs. The stamps spanned the globe—Australia, Japan, Italy, Mexico, England. One was addressed simply, "Sharon Sites—first alone transpacific woman—Hawaii." Another read, "Mrs. Sharon Sites (who sailed to Hawaii alone) Los Angeles, California." It found me in Kauai a week after my arrival.

One avid boatman, a total stranger to me, had written to President Johnson for my benefit, asking his help in getting the coast guard to change *Sea Sharp*'s rigging from a sloop, with one mast, to a two-masted yawl. That would afford easy sail trimming for the single-hander, and the boat would stick to a compass course despite minor wind variations. When I arrived in Honolulu, the man informed me of the coast guard's reply. The letter reiterated that I had been informed my journey was considered extremely hazardous and that I had been advised to reconsider my plans. I had also been advised that in the event of a mishap, my only hope would have been the chance passing of another vessel. In spite of that, I had chosen to sail anyway. The coast guard, the letter affirmed, has no authority to prevent the voluntary sailing of any U.S. citizen or to prescribe the rigging of a vessel on an offshore voyage. The coast guard appreciated the man's interest in my safety but was unable to accept his offer of advice. The letter was signed by a vice admiral of the U.S. Coast Guard, the same officer who had signed the first letter. How ironic, he seemed to have been transferred to Hawaii while I was under sail.

So much for the man's idea, though it was a nice sentiment. Obviously the coast guard still thought me foolish for making the journey.

While resting and recovering in Hawaii, I got a call from the president of Coca-Cola–Honolulu. He wanted to meet on my boat, to retrieve the Coke bottles I had saved through the journey. He made a big production, taking pictures and paying me the twelve-cent deposit due. The Coca-Cola–West Coast representative who had given me the soda in California kept a collection of bottles with unusual and interesting histories. He had a new home under construction in the desert and wanted to build a fireplace with one of those bottles in it. One bottle would be kept in Honolulu, and another would go to the owner of the Coca-Cola plant on Kauai. The remainders would head to Coca-Cola headquarters in Atlanta, the city where the drink was first served at the Jacob's Pharmacy soda fountain in May 1886. For all I know, my little transpacific bottles remain in a museum there today.

When my land legs were fully recovered and ready to go, I toured the islands for several days. I went marlin fishing on a boat just like the one that had found me. I flew to the Big Island and marveled at the black sand beaches and lava beds, massive black coils that have inundated homes and roads. In Hawaii the highway ends where lava begins; street signs and painted lines disappear beneath the flow.

On Kauai I visited Hanalei, where *South Pacific* was filmed and Waimea Canyon, a mile wide and more than three thousand feet deep. It's the largest canyon in the Pacific, a marvel of rainbow-colored crags and gorges, nooks and crannies, carved by ancient floods and storms. It's little wonder Mark Twain dubbed it "the Grand Canyon of the Pacific."

On Maui I drove the precipitous Haleakala Highway to the summit at ten thousand feet, where crowds gather for sunrise and spectacular views over the crater below. And I toured Old Lahaina, site of an 1800s whaling village.

But soon, it was time to put *Sea Sharp* to bed. I couldn't live like a tourist forever. I would have to ship the boat home to California, since I wasn't exactly ready to sail her back. Passage was arranged on a 250-foot lumber barge. She was taken to the Ala Wai boatyard, where a cradle was built for her expedition. One of the Transpac racing yachts, an unfortunate victim of demasting, would keep her company on the voyage home. That boat would return as a disabled Pacific veteran, but my little *Sea Sharp* would travel in shipshape working order—though she did look naked without her mast and rigging, pulpits, lifelines, and stanchions, which were all removed for shipping. I barely recognized her, stripped of her markings. We had grown so close, that boat and I; I thought of her as a friend. I worried about her journey without me.

When the time came, she was floated in her cradle to the main harbor and a cargo crane lifted her to the barge. She looked like a toy beside that massive, hulking vessel.

It took thirty-nine days to arrive in Hawaii from Marina del Rey.

It took *Sea Sharp* twelve days to return home on that barge.

It took me five hours by jet.

PART TWO

Adventure on Water

EIGHT

South Pacific Interlude

B oats became my life 24-7, as they say. But fame, short-lived as mine was, doesn't always breed fortune, and I couldn't afford to keep *Sea Sharp*. I sold her to a pleasant young couple just learning to sail. They wanted *Sea Sharp* for what she was and where she had been, and they paid $5,000 for her shortly after our return to California. I started work at the sailing school, cleaning and maintaining clients' boats. Suddenly without my own, I instead sailed other people's vessels up and down the California coast.

Then one day in the autumn of 1965, opportunity came. A retired Hollywood cameraman contacted Al and me about sailing around the world on a heavy wooden ketch named *Maria*. It was to be a three-year journey. The cameraman wanted to make a documentary at sea. He had the boat, he had the money, but he had no know-how for sailing. So he invited us.

In those days, an unmarried woman didn't just gallivant around the globe with a man who wasn't her husband. So Al and I were married by the same minister who had dedicated a service to me before my departure for Hawaii. It was a quick and simple ceremony, with six friends in attendance, but it gave us all the sanction we needed to begin planning our expedition at sea.

It was up to me to arrange food, so I stocked for sixty days, knowing we would be resupplying at our intended stops. We set sail for Hawaii in May. Our crew consisted of Al and me, the owner (I'll call him Bill), and Bill's buddy (I'll call him Tom), who would join us for the Hawaii leg of our journey before flying home. About ten days out, Bill got sick, gravely sick, after getting into a pot of jam. He had neglected to tell us he was diabetic. So there we were with no land in sight, our captain nearly comatose, and no doctor within two thousand miles. *Maria* was a heavy cruising boat, not capable of racing speed, but we sailed her as fast as we could to reach the islands.

This only added to the tension already on board. Let me tell you: one woman and three men is not a good recipe for a boat in the ocean. I didn't like all those egos. The agreed-upon routine was such that each person would take his or her turn with meals, though I planned the menus. What a joke! I had to clean the stove and galley each time it was my turn to cook, such a mess the guys had left before me. In addition, each of us was supposed to clean the head after using it. Guess what? We were not a compatible foursome.

Tom had come prepared with a sextant and a yellow legal pad, and he was out shooting the sun all the time. Then he'd go below and scribble figures all over his pad. I'd ask him what he learned, but he never told me. Ever.

Bill gradually recovered enough to keep watch on the boat, so we all took turns. One night about two-thirds of the way to Hawaii, I ended my routine watch at midnight and went to bed. At 2:30 a.m. one of the guys roused me; they were having a meeting and wanted me to come up. I was cranky. When a sailor is standing watch like that, on-again, off-again, she gets tired.

I went up to the cockpit and sat down by the guys.

"What's up?" I asked.

"Are you sure of our position?" they asked me.

"You're questioning?" I didn't like the sound of this. After all, I was the only one aboard with previous navigation experience. To Hawaii. Alone.

"Yes," they said. They were questioning my judgment. Tom had determined we were 180 miles off course and we would miss the islands.

"Oh really?" I asked. "Has anyone on this boat navigated before?" (I didn't state the obvious, "besides me.")

"No."

"Has anyone on this boat found the islands before?" (Again I thought, "besides me.")

There was no answer.

"Well, I'm going back to bed," I told them. "You let me know in the morning who's navigator."

I don't know what dickering they did, but in the morning, it had been decided that I would still be navigator. I figured out later that Bill and Tom were standing watch together because neither had enough sailing experience to work alone.

One thing about navigation: it starts with dead reckoning, what you think you did. And you have to be honest with yourself. Let's say you wanted to go 230 degrees, but the wind only let you do 200 degrees. There's no point in writing down 230 degrees if you only went 200 degrees, because it would be all wrong. Well, it turns out while standing watch, Bill and Tom routinely wrote down what I had asked them to do (the progress we had hoped to make), not what the boat actually had done. So every day when I took over, the numbers were off. In the end, I always managed to figure out where we really were. (Al, by the way, had never learned to navigate but often gave the impression he had. So he fluttered around the edges of these navigation debates.)

The fellows and I starting talking to each other again eventually, but they never did admit they couldn't navigate. It didn't matter. I knew I could. And I knew exactly when we'd spot Diamond Head.

It took twenty-one days for *Maria* to get us to Hawaii, and once there, Bill checked into the hospital. When he had recuperated enough to make plans, he arranged for an immediate shipment of his boat back to California. He was sick, and he wasn't going any farther. You'd think he would have known his own limitations; he had suffered from diabetes for years. But that jam had tempted him, and he was off on a fling. I suppose he thought he'd risk it.

I never saw Bill again after he departed Honolulu. As for Al and me, that was the end of our three-year tour. Before *Maria* was deck loaded for shipping back to Marina del Rey, Al and I crated and shipped our belongings home. But I wasn't going back. No way. I had prepared myself for three years at sea. I had sold my car as well as some furniture. I wasn't going home without something to show for all my talk and plans. I had a small blue drawstring duffel bag, which I still have today and show off when I give public presentations about my sailing years. I packed that bag, my camera, and purse, and I set off with Al to see the world. I suppose you could have called me a duffler—the backpack, or backpacker, phenomenon had yet to be born.

So Al and I flew to Tahiti, hoping to find work as crew on other people's boats. We took an interisland supply boat to Bora Bora and stayed in a one-room shack a few miles out of town, if you could call it a town. In those days, there were no hotels, no resorts like the monstrosities that exist now. The shack had a dirt floor, thatched roof, hammocks for beds, cupboards made from apple boxes, no water, and no bath. We lugged jugs of water from the village on our rented bicycles. We cooked over an open fire outside, between the front of the hut and the Pacific Ocean, a sight so beautiful you wouldn't believe me. We paid about $6 for one week's stay.

We easily made friends with the natives. I remember a kind gentleman who had elephantiasis. He took a liking to me and followed me like a puppy dog. He wove me a hat and made me a necklace of cowrie shells. We couldn't speak to each other except through smiles and pictures in the sand. One morning when I awoke and stepped outside, he was there holding a fresh squid, which he had caught for my breakfast. Not exactly what I wanted, but I gladly accepted his hospitality.

The next cargo boat went to American Samoa, a straight shot northwest. As I remember, it was about a $3 fare—but then your "accommodations" were the deck space it took to unroll your woven mat, much like the Alaskan ferries today minus the need for hot cocoa and long johns. Samoa was a place with such friendly locals we couldn't walk the streets. We'd be pulled into every hut along the way, given tea, and asked to chat about the world. They were the most wonderful people, but we just couldn't get very far with so many hospitable hands guiding us in every direction.

There in Samoa, I happened to visit the room where Captain Eddie Rickenbacker recovered from his tribulations at sea. In October 1942 the pilot had been sent on a mission to deliver a message to General Douglas MacArthur on Canton Island. His plane hit a tailwind that caused the aircraft to drift off course. Rickenbacker missed Canton, and he and his crew had to ditch the plane at sea when they ran out of fuel. For twenty-four days, Rickenbacker and his crew drifted in rafts, surviving on rainwater, a seagull, and a few fish. American servicemen finally spotted the men near the Ellice Islands, now known as Tuvalu, midway between Hawaii and Australia. Rickenbacker was taken to an American military hospital in Samoa, which was later turned into apartments. And that's the place I visited. I met a generous

American couple there, and they donated three books to my little library at sea. Best of all was their donation of Joshua Slocum's *Sailing Alone Around the World*.

From there Al and I sailed through Western Samoa and on to Suva, the capital of Fiji, where we met the Schiffs, a family from Rancho Palos Verdes, California. They owned a ninety-one-foot ketch, the *Sans Souci* (which means "without care"), and they needed someone to help with the sailing and chores. Bingo! Precisely the opportunity we'd hoped for. *Sans Souci* was in the boatyard having her bottom cleaned, and she would be out of commission for a month. That left us four weeks of playtime. Al and I caught a Japanese freighter to New Caledonia and New Zealand.

Things happen when you travel, little moments of serendipity. There seems to be a whole community of travelers, scattered around the globe yet operating on the same wavelength. The same universe. It's a fraternity (or sorority), really, of people who gravitate toward the nomadic life. On that freighter, we met a woman from New Zealand who had lived in Rhodesia for years. She had a car that she never drove. It needed driving. So she gave us the keys and sent us on tour. A German car, Rhodesian plates, driven by Americans in New Zealand.

We visited the Maori villages. Wonderful villages. The Maori expressed their myths and legends in carvings and weavings. Everything was carved. They carved canoes, instruments, weapons. Every carving depicted an element of history or a story of the ancestors. They carved anything and everything that could be made of wood. They lived in carved houses; they draped carvings around their necks. As an oral culture, the Maori spoke and whittled their traditions. I remember watching an elderly wood-carver shaping a goddess of the sea, called Totara, which he gave me as a gift. I still have that figurine, about five inches tall with inset abalone-shell eyes.

And who could forget Waitomo, home of the Glowworm Caves, one of the wonders of the world. To get there, visitors were led through total darkness, clinging to a railing, before boarding a small boat. A guide pulled each boat into the caves by a static line. In absolute silence, those magical glowworms illuminated the giant caves. But the slightest noise instantaneously snuffed their light. It made you want to hold your breath, just to keep the light alive.

We spent three weeks in New Zealand before returning to Fiji. With several days remaining before setting sail on the *Sans Souci*, we explored. The islands survive on sugarcane, which had been introduced in the 1880s. Over the next forty years, tens of thousands of indentured servants were brought from India to work in the fields. Indentured labor ended by 1920, but the Indians remained. When I was there, they still harvested the sugarcane and fueled the islands' economy.

An East Indian family served one of the most memorable meals of my travels. It was a Sunday afternoon, and I was walking down a country sort of lane. A young man in shorts and T-shirt descended from his house on a little hill. He invited me up for dinner. He took me into a bustling cookhouse and introduced me to his mother and sisters, all dressed in traditional saris. He spoke a little English and was very proud to be acting as interpreter. The cooking area was a separate room made of adobe, with a dirt floor and a fireplace, not very modern. The dining hall was a screened porch that ran the length of the house. There, the extended family of men, ten or twelve in all, sat at the table and ate the food that had been cooked and served by the women. Aside from myself, no woman was invited to stay; such was their custom.

There was a wash sink just inside the door, and the men ate with their hands. I made a mess of myself, but I kept eating and eating and eating: curries and chutney, soup and rice, fish and marinated meats. I wish I could remember the dishes better. I've never found them again, though I've tried many Indian restaurants since then, looking for those flavors; but nothing tastes the same. Nothing tastes as good as it did that Sunday afternoon on the screened porch of a thatched home on a small tropical island in the middle of the Pacific.

We boarded the *Sans Souci*, looking forward to new adventures, knowing we would be seeing places no tourist ever sees. Al and I joined nine others: the owner, Eric; his wife, Betty; their four children, Aries, Ricky, Marina, and Emile; and two Fijians, Osea and Roy. In addition, a relative of the Schiffs joined us for a few weeks before flying home. Compared with my hermit life aboard *Sea Sharp*, we had a small town there on the *Sans Souci*.

Osea had a university education, so he took over tutoring the children with their correspondence courses, relieving Betty of that chore. When the children eventually returned to their schools, they were ahead of their classmates, plus they had all the added education of travel—lessons that no textbook could afford.

The Schiffs had been on water already for two years, sailing throughout the South Pacific that entire time. There's more than enough to explore. The boat had had a complete makeover before she left California; this was no slipshod operation. There was a main salon plus a dining salon with a gimbaled table big enough to seat all of us. There were five staterooms, three full heads, a bathtub for the Schiffs, and a shower for us. The Fijians had a toilet and sink in the bow, and they bathed in the sea.

The Schiffs tried to bring household comforts aboard. That boat had one gadget after another, but most eventually failed. They managed to keep the freezer and hot water running, but the washing machine and water maker both died. Motors and salt air are not easily compatible. Eric had a shortwave ham radio, so he could call to San Francisco every now and then when the weather was right and so he could have parts sent to our next port of call. Their idea of cruising was an entirely different breed from the bare-bones single-handing I'd done the year before.

At sea I was assistant navigator and stood watch from 4:00 a.m. to 8:00 a.m. Under sail, I also cooked lunch. The Schiffs didn't pay us and we didn't pay them, such was our arrangement. They furnished the food; we paid for our own extras. All that time I was gone, I spent a whopping $800—a few tickets, numerous rolls of film, various incidentals, and the material for a couple of simple dresses I wore ashore. Betty and I traded days cooking when we were at anchor, so when I wanted to travel, to be gone a few days, it was OK. She never wanted to be too far from the boat or the children, so she didn't venture out much.

There were so many islands; Fiji alone has 332. Such idyllic places. On the little isle of Laluka, Eric even inquired whether it was for sale (no luck). Once we cleared customs, we could just go, go, go, from one island to the next, wherever we pleased. Sometimes we stopped at an uncharted harbor, though not often. It was hard to maneuver and anchor without a chart. Everyone lined up at the bow, searching for coral heads as Eric inched slowly ahead.

One day, we sailed into a lagoon, and before we dropped anchor, a couple of outriggers came to greet us, two men in each boat paddling fast. Were we welcome? We sure hoped so. That was on the island of Kandavu. The natives took a lot of interest in us. They didn't get many light-skinned visitors, though we could see there had been a few during World War II—blondes and redheads mixed in the crowds, and scraps of war relics lying about.

It was Sunday, so some of us went to the little native church. They sat us in the front row and gave us a welcome in English. We put a pound note into the collection basket, and the villagers were astounded. Everything else was pennies. We didn't understand the rest of the service, but the setting inspired us.

Inside the church were flower vases made of artillery shell casings, leftovers from the war that were kept polished and shiny. The school bell was a bomb casing hanging from a tree. When the children struck that bell with sticks, it produced a beautiful but ironic resonance.

It started blowing pretty hard that afternoon, and since we were afraid of dragging anchor, we moved around to Kavala Bay, the prettiest we'd yet seen. There were villages scattered through the area, each very poor. We told the people we hoped to stay a few days, and for that privilege, we traded a box of brown sugar, a pound of margarine, and a box of Cream of Wheat. A little while later, several locals came to us carrying a nice fat pig, hogtied with its feet bound together over a pole. Our two Fijian crew members knew precisely what to do. We spent that whole day preparing a luau, building a pit, and roasting that pig. One of the locals broke open a coconut, removed the shell, took the meat of the fruit, wrapped it in the coconut fiber, and wrung it like a towel. He had the strength of a giant, the hands of a hulk. Then he stirred onions and chopped cabbage into the coconut milk. The mixture was buried in the fire in a covered metal bowl and cooked with the pig, and it resulted in the best cabbage and onions I'd ever tasted. We ate a feast that day, lying on hand-woven mats in the sand.

The next day, Eric and Aries went ashore and returned with a newly hatched parrot they had found abandoned on the ground. It was a brown mass of fluff that couldn't even hold its head up. We all thought it would be dead within a few hours, but how wrong we were. Betty and I played momma parrot, trying to find something to feed the poor bird. We made gruel, added a bit of honey, and fed it with an eyedropper every few hours. It was like having a baby aboard; whoever was on watch was responsible for feeding duties. The boys named him Jib, and he grew into a brilliant little fellow. He seemed to love living aboard and became a fixture of the boat. He hung around for quite some time, too, and the Schiffs planned on taking him home to California. But then one day, as

Betty sat on deck visiting with a neighboring yacht, poor Jib flew off and fell into the water. Before anyone could get him out, he had drowned, poor bird.

Sometimes it seemed we were running our own aid ship. One day, Osea found an old man who had stuck a stick in one eye and was really hurting. There wasn't much in the way of medical care nearby. He had nothing with which to treat it. We made a trip through a mangrove swamp to take him some antibiotics, eye drops, and sterile pads. He was grateful for the help, but all we could offer in the long run was hope.

Next stop: New Hebrides, now known as Vanuatu. At that time, the islands were lumped into an Anglo-French "condominium," governed jointly by the British and French. That meant two New Hebrides communities, one English-speaking, the other French-speaking. It also meant, for our purposes, two sets of customs and immigration, two forms of money, two sets of laws, two spools of red tape. I don't know how the residents knew who was governing them.

First, we stopped at Pentecost Island, which I'd seen in *National Geographic*. It was the time of year when the natives performed an ancient bungee-jumping ritual called the Naghol. The men made wooden towers several stories tall and dived from the top with vines tied to their ankles. It's an ancient form of bungee jumping, done over land. Legend has it that the first diver was a woman escaping her abusive husband. She climbed a large banyan and he followed. She jumped and so did he, not knowing she had tied a vine to her ankles. The wife survived—the husband didn't. And for years afterward, women carried out this ritual, until tribal elders decided men should perform the diving duties to redress their shame and promote a decent yam harvest. These days, of course, the Naghol ceremony is Pentecost's number-one tourist attraction, and a brutal one at that. When the dive goes awry, the men break their ankles or smash their heads. Some divers never walk away.

Next, we arrived at the island of Malekula just in time for a celebration. The community had cleared an "airstrip," though no one had ever landed there. That day would be the first. A British airplane was scheduled to arrive with six people and supplies for the island, which was home to a Catholic mission. So the native tribe, the Nambas, came to greet the winged visitors. The Nambas were divided into two subgroups, big and small, and they were famous for one thing: the penis sheath all men traditionally wore—the only thing they wore. Suffice it to say, those men with the biggest sheaths were called the "Big Nambas," and those less endowed (in sheath) were the "Little Nambas."

On that celebratory day, however, Catholic nuns would be in attendance, so for modesty's sake, the Nambas men covered their backsides with fans made from leaves and coated their skin in pig grease and ashes. They wore anklets of seedpods that jangled when they danced. The planes brought each tribesman a hunk of cow meat, a heap of bananas, and other supplies to take to their village in the mountains.

To this day, I can't recall how it happened, but we were invited to a Nambas village, a long trek from shore. By that time, the tribesmen frequently came down from the hills and out of the jungles to sell little carved trinkets to the interisland boats that stopped at Malekula. But a century earlier, we were told, the Nambas had been the most ferocious of the island cannibal tribes. So ferocious, the entire region was named the Cannibal Islands. In years past, it had been a long-standing joke among Catholic missionaries that the Nambas preferred the flavor of Methodists.

So Eric, Al, and I hiked to a Nambas village, which looked to me like a mouse maze enclosed with bamboo fencing, presumably built that way for self-defense. We walked through a series of long, narrow walkways, which dead-ended when we had chosen the wrong path. We backtracked and did it again until we got to the center of the maze.

When we arrived, one of the village leaders greeted us and took us to meet the chief. The man kept rubbing his head, as though he had a terrible headache, so I took some aspirin from my purse and made motions for him to swallow it. Presto—a convert to modern medicine.

The villagers wanted to show their appreciation for our coming to their village, so they prepared a ceremony. There was a clearing in the dirt about thirty feet wide. Five men sat in a crescent in the dirt, the same dirt trampled by pigs, dogs, and people. The three of us sat across from them. The Nambas man in the middle had a carved piece of wood, a bowl of sorts. He had several half-coconut shells and a pile of dirty roots. (They looked like dirty parsnips to me; I hate parsnips.) The ceremony began, and I could see, I could sense, what was coming. I kept thinking of the times I had to swallow bad medicine as a child: throw my head back, open my throat, and take it in one gulp. That's all I could think, besides a silent prayer: Lord, please let it go down and stay down.

Twenty minutes passed, then thirty, then forty. The men did some rhythmic clapping and made chanting noises that sounded like *booola booola* to my foreign ears. The man in the middle called to a little boy off to the side, who jumped up and returned with a piece of bamboo, three feet long and wide enough for a baseball to fit inside. The bamboo was full of water and squiggly bugs, which the boy poured into the bowl. The man stirred the water and roots with his hands. I knew the time had arrived.

It turned out that the man in the middle was the chief chewer. He stuck the dirty roots into his mouth and chewed and chewed, then spat them back into the bowl. Then he dipped one of the coconut shells into the masticated liquid and held it out for me to drink.

I did the only thing I could: I pretended I was a child again, tossed my head back, and swallowed.

My mouth was instantly numb. It felt as though I'd been to the dentist and my tongue and cheeks were just beginning to emerge from novocaine. I think that's what saved me. I think that's why it stayed down. I never did learn exactly what I'd swallowed. It was awful—obviously some sort of narcotic—but I survived no worse for the experience.

When we returned from the Nambas village, the missionaries told us about another group high in the mountains. The village had no name; it was simply known as the place where "the pig people" lived. None of the missionaries had been there, and the villagers never came down. No outsiders had hoofed up those hills in fourteen years, not since a geology team had gone off surveying and one of the team members hadn't returned. People presumed, of course, the man had been killed; perhaps so. There were no trails to the village. But the nuns knew someone who spoke a little pidgin English, and that person knew someone who knew where the tribe lived.

I was intrigued; I just had to go, even if no one would go with me. In the end, Al consented, and we took a couple of native guides. I packed my blue duffel bag and five days of food and water, and off we set to find the pig people.

The trail was thick with rainforest, and I followed our guides who whacked at trees and vines, slashing their way. The air dripped with heat and humidity. The ground rolled beneath our feet. I looked down as I trudged, and I walked straight into a spider as big as a tennis ball. Our trek continued that way, through miles and miles of rugged terrain.

By midmorning on the second day, we came to a little clearing. Our guide motioned for us to stay put. While our guide continued on, the rest of us waited, hoping we had correctly understood.

We had. The guide returned a while later, shaking his head.

What did that mean? Whatever the question, his answer was no. We walked on.

A little while later, the leader took us to another clearing and left again. We waited. Soon I knew we were being watched; I could feel it in the hairs on my neck. We seemed to be alone, but I could feel eyes upon us. I stood there in that jungle clearing like a strange ghost in my long, white jeans; sleeveless, high-neck blouse; bare arms; and strawberry blonde hair.

Slowly, a naked man stepped from the edge of the forest. Then another and another. They moved with caution—one step closer, waiting to see my reaction, one step closer still, then inch by inch until they were all around me within arm's reach. I heard grunting sounds made among them, but it was nothing that sounded like a language to me.

One man reached out and ran his hand down my arm, my smooth, white skin—theirs was dark and full of scabbies. I didn't do anything, just stood with hands at my sides, looking them in the eyes, smiling. Soon, the others touched me, too, until everyone in the group had had a feel—about forty men in all.

I had a pocket full of balloons. I never went anywhere without them; kids loved them. So I just started blowing up the balloons and tying them off and bouncing them with my hand.

"Ahhhhhhhhhhh," the men crowed. But they didn't smile.

I bounced the balloons from my hand to theirs, and the men caught on quickly. They bounced the balloons from one hand to another to another, and I could tell they were having great fun. But they still didn't smile.

And then one of the balloons broke. BANG!

Everyone turned to me and stared. Where did it go? What was it? That noise? They looked at me as though I were the wicked white witch. They had played so nicely; then, suddenly it was gone. I didn't know what to do. I continued to blow more balloons, and when more balloons eventually broke, the men looked at me with frightened eyes every time, though they began to see that no harm would come.

Eventually the men took us into their hut, which was a very simple thatch and bamboo A-frame. They all lived in the same house, though I saw no women. I figured they must have hidden them. In fact, in all the time I spent with those villagers, I caught only one brief glimpse of a single woman behind a tree as we were leaving.

There was a fire pit in the middle of the house, which probably had been burning for many years. The ceiling was black from ages of smoke. The villagers didn't appear to have a mealtime, though. They didn't appear to have much to eat except jungle roots and vegetables, roasted in the fire. I never saw a water supply—no stream, no lake. The jungle was thick with vines and leaves, and it rained a little every day. That was the only water I saw. They would drink from large leaves that held, maybe, a cup at a time. If that was it, I don't know how they survived. There wasn't even the sign of a coconut shell, or any utensils. No machete or axe. Just sharp sticks and stones.

We stayed the night. Someone was always near me watching EVERYTHING I did. Can you imagine what went through their minds when I opened a can of tuna? I was put to sleep on the floor near the entrance. There were only enough sleeping places for the men, so I had to assume the women had another hut close by.

The men coughed all night long in the smoky air. They lay on bamboo a foot above the ground, and they placed ashes from the fire beneath their beds, presumably to keep warm and to keep bugs at bay. I had brought a small blanket, which I pulled over my head. A rat ran across it. The critter must have been eight inches long. Let's just say I didn't sleep much that night.

The next morning, I looked up to the ceiling of that hut and saw something I knew I must have for myself. Then, I went looking for the chief.

When I found him, I took out a little dime-store mirror from a small stash of trading trinkets I had brought along. I made motions that I wanted a trade and handed him the mirror. Nothing! His face was blank. He was seeing a stranger; it was obvious he had never seen his own reflection before.

Then, another man took the mirror and looked. Nothing. No sign of recognition. He passed it on to another man. Nothing. Finally, one man took the mirror and looked at his face just as several flies had landed on it. He slapped his hand at the flies and saw the scene simultaneously revealed in the mirror. He slapped himself again and his eyes lit up. He understood.

The mirror quickly made the rounds again, and this time each man was slapping his face, watching himself do it, then doing it again.

So the mirror became a big hit. I traded it for a wild boar's tusk, black as the ace of spades. The Nambas had many of them hanging from the ceiling. Most were the typical three-quarters of a circle, but the one I wanted was a complete loop with the tooth burying itself into the jawbone a second time. The nuns informed me later that when a tooth grows this way, the women have to masticate food and spit into the boar's mouth because the boar can't forage for its food. The tooth is one of my favorite souvenirs, and it goes with me whenever I tell this story.

We left the village with no fanfare, no pictures. I didn't want to do anything to threaten or upset the pig people. We stayed thirty hours then hiked back to the harbor. I know it was different in that day; cannibalism had purportedly died out with the influence of missionaries. But it had been only a few years earlier that Michael Rockefeller disappeared while on expedition in New Guinea. His body was never found, and some speculated he was killed by cannibals. I wanted to leave on the best and quietest of terms.

I had one more adventure in the New Hebrides. The *Sans Souci* had moved on to a coconut plantation with a couple from New

Zealand. We were learning about growing coconuts and making copra, when along came an English geologist. He had heard about our boat. It's amazing, the grapevine in the South Pacific, the way messages get around. He needed to get to the island of Ambrym, about a twenty-four-hour sail away, and he didn't have a ride. Could we take him? Marum volcano was erupting. It wasn't spewing lava but puffing plumes of sulphur and ash twelve thousand feet into the air. The geologist was commissioned by the government to study the situation and to help determine whether or not to evacuate the island.

Sure, we'd take him, his five porters, and all his equipment. They all slept on deck.

As soon as we anchored and went ashore, the geologist told me I couldn't go because I wouldn't keep up. He sure didn't know me very well.

"I'm going," I insisted. "If I can't keep up, I'll come back."

When going ashore, it was always a problem wearing shoes after long periods on the boat with only flip-flops. This time I had to wear a new pair of deck shoes, oh my; but I quickly packed my little blue duffel and was the first person ready to go.

We started out, and the first day went fine. But by the second day, I had blisters so bad they bled through my shoes. Without saying a word to me, one of the porters came over to me, sat me down, and cut holes into my shoes with his machete. This gave my blisters room to breathe, relieving the pain. For the rest of the hike, that man was my self-designated protector.

As we drew closer to the base of the volcano, we reached a forest of boulders, massive boulders the size of cars. These rocks stood taller than I did. I knew I wouldn't be able to climb them. But my native friend placed his hand on my tush and hoisted me up. Up and up the mountainside we went. As we climbed higher and higher, the rocks got smaller and smaller until the ground near the top was nothing but powder, fine as talcum. When we reached the rim, I sat with one leg on the inside and the other leg on the outside. It felt like an earthquake rumbling beneath me each time it sputtered, about every fifteen minutes. And every time it rumbled, a little bit of the mountain would cave inside. Sulphur soared upward, and just as it would clear, we could see red roiling lava deep inside.

That was enough for me; it was more than the porters could take. They dropped everything and fled in fright, leaving us to help carry the geologist's instruments. The geologist told us he would recommend evacuating that end of the island.

Far less dramatic but interesting nonetheless, we stopped at Palmyra, in the middle of the Pacific about five degrees north of the equator. It had been a staging and supply area during World War II when the U.S. Navy kept a base there. We found it much as the military had left it. A "yacht club" sign hung askew over a decrepit building at the end of the dock where we tied up. Military barracks still stood with mattresses on the floor, and calendars hung on the walls with Xs marking off the days until the servicemen would go home. Concrete gun bunkers faced the sea, and the island was littered with equipment that I suppose was too ragged and rusted to take home—rusted jeeps, a fire engine, small parts, and machinery of all kinds.

Palmyra wasn't so famous when we saw it, but it would be. About seven years later it became the noted location of the gruesome but true murder-robbery thriller *And the Sea Will Tell* by Vincent Bugliosi. He wrote that the atoll was virtually flat, never reaching higher than six feet, "a horseshoe curve of more than a dozen islets spaced like jewels around a necklace protecting the lagoon. Each, hard sand and growing coral, carpeted with growth of shrubs and coconut palms."

What memories I have! I recall huge crabs, giant crabs, with one monster claw big enough to yank your ankle. Best to keep away from those. I remember, too, the lagoons we saw, so clear the bottom was visible straight through. We could follow the stingrays that came alongside the boat to check us out. And every evening at dusk, the skies would darken momentarily with thousands of white terns coming en masse to roost in the palm trees.

By that point, the boat no longer had the luxuries of hot water or frozen food. The heater and freezer had quit, so we cooked on land at night by flashlight, a glorious experience. But it had been more than a year since we left Marina del Rey—a long time on water. So we weren't too disappointed that each hop *Sans Souci* made was a step toward home.

Heading that way, we stopped at Canton, part of Kiribati, roughly midway between Fiji and Hawaii. Canton was a U.S. tracking station with men who shuttled between the island and home, six weeks here, six weeks there. They were delighted to see anyone from the outside world.

I have two sharp memories of those days in Canton. Three, actually: Lettuce, ice cream, and turtles. We had not eaten lettuce or ice cream for months, and oh boy, did we indulge.

The turtles came by the light of a full moon. During a clear night's walk along the beach, we found what looked to be army-tank treads leading toward the water. But it was no tank, just a mother turtle who had laid her eggs in sand and made her way back to the sea.

We saw the eggs starting to hatch, hundreds of two-inch baby turtles frantically following nature's urge to find water. The moon was so bright that night, we could see plainly as land crabs and sea birds came charging in for an attack. I couldn't help myself, scaring off as many predators as I could. I don't know how much I upset the laws of nature that night, but I did save dozens of turtles.

The first thing we did upon our arrival in Hawaii was check into a hotel overnight so *Sans Souci* could be fumigated. No matter how meticulous one is with provisions, there will always be those nasty little insects of the Blattodea order: cockroaches, or *cucurachas*. Call them what you will, there are at least 3,500 varieties in the world, and our fair share found their way aboard. You get used to them; you accept them. They are a fact of seafaring life in the South Pacific. We might be having lunch at the dining table, and invariably, one would scurry by and someone would remark, "There goes George again."

So we fumigated, rested up, stocked up, and fixed what was broken before heading on the final stretch toward home.

Los Angeles Harbor. We sailed right into her arms that fall, right back into the world of highways and skyscrapers, telephones and quickly ticking clocks—the world we each had left many months before.

There was no fanfare, no welcoming committee upon our return. The next day was spent unloading our things and saying goodbye. We parted, heading our separate ways, the Schiffs returning to Palos Verdes and Al and I to Marina del Rey. We all promised we would get together, swap tales, and relive our adventures at sea. But it never happened. It's always the same. Old habits quickly return, as does the hectic pace of ordinary life on land. We never did get together again. There just didn't seem to be time.

NINE

Queen Mary to Hollywood

One day shortly after our return from the South Pacific, a lady friend of Al's came to our house all excited. She had dropped my name and managed to get the three of us passenger tickets for a portion of the *Queen Mary*'s last voyage. Such were the perks of having made the Sailing Hall of Fame. It was a long list of people who wanted to make that last journey, and at each port of call, some got on and some got off. The three of us would sail from Rio de Janeiro, around Cape Horn at the tip of South America, to Valparaiso, Chile. It was a snap decision, as the *Queen* already had left England en route to her final resting spot in Long Beach.

When we boarded the boat, Al introduced his friend as his "sister," but in truth, she was no relative. My marriage with Al had run aground. We journeyed together aboard the *Queen*, but I rarely saw him and his new companion except at dinner, always a formal tuxedo and cocktail-dress affair. Thank heavens the ship was big enough to lose a fellow passenger you didn't much like. Instead, I spent my time with different officers, from the bilge to the crow's nest; but I was mostly on the bridge with the navigators. I even had tea with Captain J. Treasure Jones and his wife in their suite.

The *Queen Mary* was a star Cunard cruise ship launched in 1934. She sailed the North Atlantic, between Southampton and New York, until World War II required her services and she began transporting Australian and New Zealand troops. When the war ended, she reverted to civilian duty, turning a handsome profit for the cruise line. Her last voyage began in Southampton on October 31, 1967, and ended in Long Beach, California, where she remains as a tourist attraction today.

The ship was huge, 1,019.5 feet long. Every night there was a cocktail party, and it took half an hour just to walk the length of the ship to get there from my cabin. When we boarded, they told us all manner of statistics about this extraordinary lady. She was a queen of numbers: 81,237 gross tons, two thousand portholes, ten million rivets, twelve decks, 1,957 passengers possible, 160,000 horsepower, three whistles, three smokestacks, and twenty-seven boilers. What a thrill to find myself aboard.

I remember it was hot in Rio; it must have been 110 degrees the day we departed. It was so hot, one of the ship's chefs died. Most of the crew were old-time Cunard employees; he was an older fellow, along for his final expedition at sea. The crew called the man's wife, who decreed that her husband should have a fine burial at sea. So that's what they did. There were wreaths of flowers, prayers, and bagpipe music. The body was bound in canvas and rope, weighed down, and placed on a plank beneath a flag. There was a ceremony on deck, then the crew raised the end of the plank and slid the body into the water. That was it—and I thought it a fitting way for any seaman to go.

We sailed off the coast of Argentina, where the weather chilled and it began to snow. We sailed around Cape Horn—a disappointment, I thought; it's a sheer, gray, cone-shaped rock face nearly 1,400 feet high. I don't know what I had expected, but after all the horrendous sea stories one reads about all the ships and lives lost, I guess I had imagined more than a big rock. It's not even a cape, really, but a small island called Hoorn. For centuries, sailors have despised this shard of land where winds and waters so frequently converge in tumult. When we crossed, the usual mist and clouds had raised enough to get a decent view. I stood out on the wing of the bridge for a picture with the ship's captain and his wife, with that cliff in the background.

As we rounded South America and started up the west coast of Chile the skies opened up and delivered the storm of storms. Winds blew sixty miles per hour; the seas reached fifty feet, then sixty feet, then higher. The *Queen Mary* took green water over her bow, seventy-four feet above the waterline. So often sailors talk of seas that high, and it's usually just talk. But that time, there was no exaggeration. Passengers hunkered inside, snug in their bunks; hardly a soul ventured around ship, though of course I did. I wouldn't miss the adventure.

The stabilizers were out, like fins, to counteract the ship's rolling. I could barely walk along the decks, and you can believe no one was about. No one but I. Knowing I would have a period of extremely cold weather, I had borrowed a mouton fur coat from a friend who had kept it from her college days in Michigan. I carried it all through the sweltering heat of Rio, but it sure came in handy that day on deck. The wind blew that coat straight out from my body. At times, those gusts knocked me to my knees.

We disembarked two days later at Valparaiso, along with a dozen other passengers who would go on to Machu Picchu in the high Peruvian Andes. Al, his friend, and I took the train inland to Santiago. But Santiago was having some political problems in those days. The U.S. Embassy was barricaded, and crowds rioted in the streets. Protesters threw tomatoes and rocks at the embassy. Gunfire could be heard through the city, so we didn't stay.

We went to Lima and toured the sights for several days with sailor friends we had met at the yacht club. From there, we traveled to Cuzco, the jumping-off point for Machu Picchu, that ancient retreat of the Incan nobility. Machu Picchu is a stunning site, at 12,500 feet, hovering over a precipice that drops 2,000 feet down to the Urubamba River. It was a *llacta*, a sanctuary from which the ruling elite kept control over their conquered territories. Like so many historical ruins, the "discovery" of Machu Picchu was attributed to a Western scientist, Yale archaeologist Hiram Bingham, in 1911. What once was the Lost City of the Incas is now one of South America's most popular tourist spots, drawing hundreds of thousands of visitors each year. I was fortunate to have seen it in 1967, long before world travel had become a household notion, before access was limited in order to control tourist numbers.

Our group took a train across the high Andes to Lake Titicaca, then sailed across the lake to Bolivia on the ss *Inca*, a cargo boat that had been brought up from the sea piece by piece and reassembled in 1920. It had accommodations for eight passengers in closet-size cabins.

At 12,507 feet, Titicaca is the world's highest commercially navigable lake. We took an eleven-hour circuitous route among the lake's many islands. We passed the Uros, a conglomeration of more than forty man-made islands of reeds. The Uro people moved to Titicaca centuries ago to escape the Inca, and they built their islands using the totora reeds that grow abundantly in the lake. They anchored with ropes attached to sticks staked to the lake bottom. As the reeds on the bottom of the islands grew soggy and rotten, the people cultivated new reeds and lay them down on top.

Those reed islands and their inhabitants were the subject of much scientific and geographical speculation. In a 1955 expedition to Easter Island, the adventurer and ethnographer Thor

Heyerdahl found a proliferation of the American tortora reed, similar to that of Titicaca. He had long surmised that Polynesia had been populated by people from the Americas, not Asia. To show it was possible, he sailed a balsa-wood raft, the *Kon-Tiki*, 4,300 miles from Peru to Polynesia in 1947. Heyerdahl later tried to prove that papyrus boats were seaworthy. He built two boats. The first, *Ra*, broke apart in the Atlantic. But the second, *Ra II*, which he commissioned to have built in Titicaca, he successfully sailed from Morocco to Barbados.

I, on the other hand, went from Titicaca to Bolivia, where I boarded an airplane that took me back to California. I arrived in Long Beach just as the *Queen Mary* finished her voyage. Thousands of boats went to greet her as she came in. Nine others and I were on *Firefly*, a Mariner 40, bobbing in the maelstrom of white water churned up by all those spectators around us. It was one of the most spectacular sights ever seen on water. She had taken thirty-nine days to complete the journey, just as I had from California to Hawaii.

I returned to the marina and periodically worked for Bill Harbach, producer of a variety show called *The Hollywood Palace* and owner of the *Firefly*. He wanted it to be a showboat, and it was. The linens and napkins all matched, all the right shade of blue, all mono-grammed with the *Firefly* name. Every weekend after he took the boat out, Bill would give me a call: come fix this scratch or that ding. *Firefly* wasn't mine, but I knew it from bow to stern.

Bing Crosby happened to be a friend of Bill's. When Bing had a ten-day birthday bash in Mexico in May 1968, I was asked to help sail the *Firefly* down to the party. We sailed from Los Angeles to Cabo San Lucas to Las Cruces, where Crosby had his place on the Sea of Cortez. If you wanted to fly in, you flew to nearby La Paz and Bing would send his plane to get you. Or he'd send a boat. Or you'd bring your own.

1. On *Sea Sharp*—almost ready. To the left is my first boat, *Super Sport*.
Photograph courtesy of Jason Hailey.

2. (*left*) *Sea Sharp* under sail, departing for Hawaii. Photograph courtesy of
Jason Hailey.

3. (*above*) *Sea Sharp II* on the day before my arrival in San Diego. Oberly Collection.

4. (*left*) At the Marina del Rey two weeks after reaching San Diego. Photograph courtesy of Jason Hailey.

5. (*above*) A look inside the cabin of *Sea Sharp*—note the gimbaled sterno stove and kerosene lamp. Photograph courtesy of the author.

6. (*left*) Taking a sextant sight. Photograph courtesy of the author.

7. (*top*) Surfing a following sea. Photograph courtesy of the author.

8. (*bottom*) *Sea Sharp* being shipped home from Hawaii. Photograph courtesy of the author.

9. (*left*) The masts for *Sea Sharp II* were carved by a hand adze, the old-fashioned way. Photograph courtesy of the author.

10. (*above*) Varnish drying inside the cabin of *Sea Sharp II*. Photograph courtesy of the author.

11. (*left top*) Launch day—workers prepare to install masts and spars on *Sea Sharp II*. Photograph courtesy of the author.

12. (*left bottom*) Some of the boatyard workers who put their love into *Sea Sharp II*. Photograph courtesy of the author.

13. (*above*) Heading for the open ocean—note the Plexiglas bubble and the life raft. Photograph courtesy of the author.

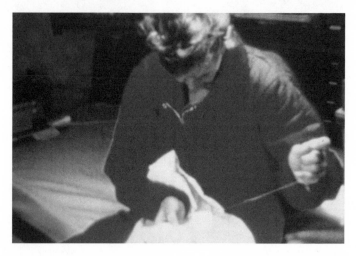

14. (*top*) Cutting out a dress to pass the time. Photograph courtesy of the author.

15. (*bottom*) Sewing the dress—note the Zenith transoceanic radio at the end of the bunk. Photograph courtesy of the author.

16. (*top*) Doing chart work under the warmth of the bubble. Photograph courtesy of the author.

17. (*bottom*) My thirty-ninth birthday party aboard *Sea Sharp II*. Photograph courtesy of the author.

18. (*top*) Mending a sail. Photograph courtesy of the author.

19. (*bottom*) Looking through the bubble. Photograph courtesy of the author.

20. (*top*) *Sea Sharp II* at sea, viewed from the deck of the *President McKinley*.

21. (*bottom*) The *President McKinley*. Photograph courtesy of the author.

22. (*top*) Gooney birds keeping me company in the doldrums. Photograph courtesy of the author.

23. (*bottom*) Tied up at home, *Sea Sharp II* tugs at her lines to be gone again. Photograph courtesy of the author.

24. *Sea Sharp II.* Photograph courtesy of the Japanese military.

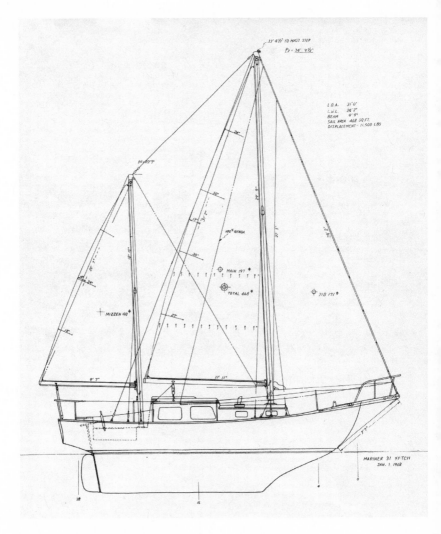

Diagram 1. Mariner 31 ketch

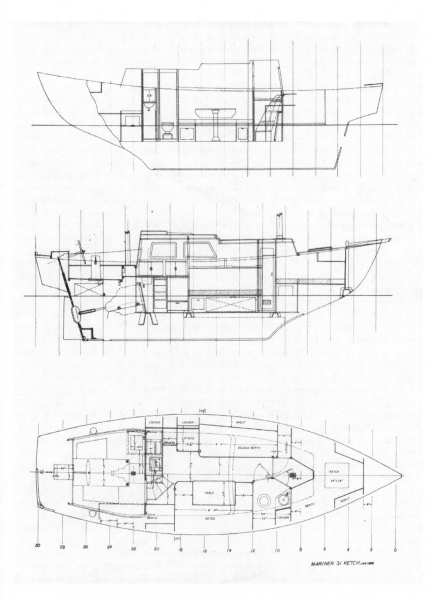

Diagram 2. *(top)* Side view of the M31

Diagram 3. *(middle)* Opposite side view of the M31

Diagram 4. *(bottom)* Top view of the M31

What better can one do in life than to get paid for something like that? To hobnob with the famous? And to eat the food of the stars? All told, it was a month of sailing and partying with people coming and going in a constant stream. I remember some of the faces and names. John Swope, a *Life* photographer, was there with his wife, Dorothy McGuire. Edgar Bergen was there with his wife. He was different in person. His stories were a little risqué, but on TV he always acted straight-laced. Henry Mancini was there. So was Dina Merrill, who was then married to Cliff Robertson.

The actual birthday party was a riot, a lively dinner with a special surprise for the birthday boy. When all the guests had gathered in the dining room, in strutted a burro in a funny hat.

It was a ten-day vacation, sun and sail. The women spent their days lying around the pool and playing tennis or golf and always wearing the right clothes. They kept changing outfits. We talked a bit; they asked me about sailing now and then. But not much. I didn't belong in their world.

There were enough guest cabins to accommodate fifty, but I slept on *Firefly* and used a little rowboat to get around. I fished a lot with Bing on his boat, one of the biggest treats of the job. He was just a down-to-earth Spokane boy when he wasn't in the spotlight. We were fishing for marlin together one day, and I just couldn't help it. I had to ask him.

"Bing, do you know your socks don't match?" He wore one green sock and one brown.

"They probably don't," he laughed. That's because he dressed himself that day. When it mattered, someone else chose his clothing for him.

Why?

"I'm color blind," he said.

PART THREE

Across the Pacific

TEN

Another *Sea Sharp*

All this time, I'd been saying I had single-handed the Pacific, but that wasn't true. I'd only sailed to Hawaii; I'd only sailed one-third of the distance. I couldn't stop thinking about that as I polished boats and moseyed around the marina.

By that time, Al and I had reached a breaking point. While I still went by the name Adams, he went off flying around the world with his lady friend. So I felt free and eager. Maybe I should try another crossing—just a thought.

But how? I had little money. I didn't even have a boat. All I had was an idea and a contact. I called up Clair Oberly, owner of Far East Boats, which I had heard and read about. I asked Clair to meet me for coffee in Long Beach on July 10, 1968.

"Would you build me a boat to sail across the Pacific?" I asked, straight to the point. Clair's company, based in Yokosuka, Japan, built yachts for export to the United States. He'd founded the company in 1957 and built half a dozen or more types of boats.

"You want to buy one of my boats?" he smiled.

"No. I just want to deliver one."

He was astounded! There was a long pause, but since he didn't say no, I kept talking. I told him what I wanted: a boat not too big, not too small, and with standing headroom and rigging for single-handing.

We drank more coffee.

He told me about the new fiberglass Mariner 31, a thirty-one-foot ketch rig with full galley, dinette, large head, lots of storage, and six feet of standing headroom.

We drank more coffee (I'm an addict). Another hour passed; he still hadn't said no. "Make a list of what you want," he told me. "We'll meet on my boat next time and talk again."

I started that list and couldn't stop. I wanted a lot: I wanted bigger winches. I wanted a furling genoa and staysail, higher double lifelines, larger pulpits, and a butane stove. I wanted a third shroud, heavier cable running rigging, and ladder rungs up the main mast so I could climb to the spreaders.

I also had two very particular requests. First, I wanted a Plexiglas bubble I could get my head and shoulders into. I had this idea that if I could stand in that bubble and see 360 degrees and assess all the rigging, I wouldn't have to go outside to check that everything was as it should be. It would be a convenient way to do the rounds without facing the elements. On the way to Hawaii, my hatch cover had been a flat piece of Plexiglas, so all I could do was look straight up. It drove me crazy. I vowed that if I ever made another crossing, I'd do something about it. I'd build myself a bubble. I contacted an acrylic fabrication machining company in Alhambra, California, which made salad bowls and such. Would they make what I wanted? It would need a lip around the edge to secure it to the boat. They said they would try.

The second desire was a reliable wind vane to steer the boat. I had never had one, but I knew many cruising boats were equipped with them. I understood that there was nothing "automatic" about a wind vane, that every time the velocity or direction of the wind changed I would have to make all new adjustments. I merely hoped the wind vane could occasionally go for hours at a time, so I wouldn't have to.

I met Clair on his boat, and I told him all of these things, all the modifications, all the additions. And I told him it might take me ninety days to get that boat across the ocean. To my astonishment, he agreed. Then he suggested a brilliant idea: since his boatyard was close to Yokohama and since that was a sister city to San Diego, he suggested contacting authorities from both cities to see if they would be interested in my crossing. Lo and behold, they were, which is how I chose the embarkation and disembarkation points of my trip. San Diego happened to be celebrating its bicentennial that year—perfect. I'd deliver something of a birthday gift from the city's sister in Japan.

For six months I made lists, four legal pads full of lists—things to do before leaving home; things I would need in Japan; things the boat would need; and things I would need on the crossing such as food, toiletries, first aid, repair parts, and oh, so much more. I even thought of the dress I would need for my first evening ashore in San Diego. I left it with my friend, Dione, to bring to me upon my arrival. To me, these lists meant survival. I was trying to preconceive what I might face for months on water so that I wouldn't forget anything vital.

The physical preparation began as well. The acrylic fabrication company made my bubble, and it turned out better than I had hoped. A designer named Pete Maruschak of Westchester, California, made my wind vane. He put together a kit of every pillow block, every piece of stainless steel tubing, nut, bolt, and washer I would need, and he included instructions for complete assembly and mounting to the transom. I looked at it and thought, "Believe me, never has a better wind vane been made."

On February 24, 1969, my plans were made public at a press conference in the San Diego mayor's office. It was official: I would sail from Yokohama, Japan, to San Diego, California.

By then, preparations for Mariner 31, hull number 27 already were underway in Yokosuka, a port town not far from Yokohama in Tokyo Bay. The fiberglass hull had been poured on Valentine's Day in a snowstorm. In freezing weather, a tent had to be constructed over her frame, and the fledgling boat was surrounded by lights and heaters so work could continue apace.

I went through the rigmarole of leaving again, updating my will, storing my car, and closing my house. This time Dr. Gold, the same doctor I'd had for years, simply said I wasn't going again with my appendix still intact. If my appendix were to burst, infection could spread easily, killing me quickly. So the appendix came out.

I flew to Japan in early March, moving into the boatyard with the bachelor boat builders. They lived in barracks that consisted of sixteen two-room apartments. One kind worker vacated his quarters, and I took his spot. I ate their food, I drank their tea, and I worked nearly as long and hard as they did—but not quite. They started at 8:00 a.m. and finished at 9:00 p.m., five full weeks of thirteen-hour days.

My Mariner had twenty-six workers looking after her. They were attentive and worked with pride. They painted meticulously, just the right shade of pink (my favorite color), sheer stripes along the water line, decks, and cabin top. Her laminated oak and ash spars were carved by a master by hand with an adze, the old-fashioned way. Her sanding and varnishing was done by women, immaculate work. Some of her hardware was made to order. I spoke no Japanese; the workers spoke no English. We communicated through sign language and drawings, and through lots of smiles and bows.

A small Perkins diesel was built into her as construction progressed, not for me to use but for Clair to have later. I had to keep reminding myself she wasn't my boat. I was just a surrogate.

Only once did the slightest bit of animosity take root in the boatyard. I told the head carpenter about the Plexiglas dome I had brought with me from California. I wanted a hole cut into the top of the cabin. He didn't like that, the equivalent of gouging a wound into and sticking a plastic bandage over the middle of his wooden masterpiece. But he eventually did it just the way I had wanted, with a teak mounting. As for the wind vane, there was no problem.

Sea Sharp II was launched on April 25, 1969, just three months after the press conference in San Diego. The U.S. Navy had given me special permission to use a small dock at its base in Yokosuka since I was, to the navy's mind, completing a mission of international friendship.

The boat had two launchings: a Japanese launch and an American launch. The boatyard manager had arranged for a Shinto priest in flowing white robes. He had bowls containing water, salt, rice, fish, and vegetables, and with each he blessed the bow, the stern, the sea, and me. He prayed and passed the boughs of a tree over me while I bowed my head and clapped three times. It was serene and beautiful, and it took forty minutes.

The American ceremony was much quicker. I broke a bottle of pink champagne over the bow with one strike, and splat went the champagne. Launching a boat is an awkward event. There's no easy way to do it. The boat had been moved on rollers to the edge of a seawall by hand. Then a crane just picked her up and lifted her over the side and placed her into the water with me aboard. That was it. The birth of a lady. I raised the Japanese flag, and the crowd cheered as I embarked on that boat's first trip—half a mile around the corner to the dock at the naval base.

In celebration that evening, the boatyard manager, the foreman, and four others hosted a dinner. "Do you want American or Japanese?" the manager asked. Japanese, of course. We were taken into the countryside to a nontouristy restaurant, where we walked through a Zen-garden entryway and left our shoes at the door. Our private room had a sliding rice-paper door, low tables, and pillows to sit on. Our servers were lovely Japanese ladies in full kimono dress. The boatyard manager chose a live fish as we entered, and later it was carried in raw, on a three-foot platter surrounded by very colorful items, all foreign to me. The fish had been killed outside the door, sliced into paper-thin strips, and served with a variety of delicious sauces. I wanted to try everything, but I didn't necessarily want to know what everything was. I told the host not to tell me unless I asked.

I still had seventeen days and a lot of work before leaving Yokohama. I had chosen May 12 as departure day because the typhoon season in that part of the world generally begins after June 1. I wanted a head start, but everything was running late. The last installment of rigging had been shipped on the wrong freighter from Los Angeles, and it arrived in Japan six weeks overdue. The final touches weren't yet complete—I needed another cleat, I needed a bolt to lock the stove in place. So many little things. I had to move myself aboard the boat, which was always an ordeal of packing and thinking, repacking and rethinking. I had had virtually no time to get my bearings, to get a good feel for *Sea Sharp II*'s ways. I worried about crossing the ocean on an unfamiliar boat.

Though our marriage had fizzled, Al remained one of the most knowledgeable sailors I knew, and he agreed to help me with preparations. I bought him an airline ticket so he could come over to teach me how to use the wind vane and help with the final rigging. Ordinarily, Mariners were not rigged in Japan. They were loaded onto freighters and finished in Newport, California.

Well, now I was growing worried because Al hadn't been able

to get that wonderful, custom-built wind vane to work for more than twenty minutes in Tokyo Bay. What could I do? Why didn't it work? No one could steer six thousand miles.

I worried, too, about handling the mainsail in storms and heavy seas. The main boom weighed almost as much as I did. Too much to handle!

I hadn't taken the boat out enough. Every time I wanted to sail, a reporter was on the phone or at the docks looking for an interview. Not that I knocked publicity; I appreciated every word I had. But those men—almost all of them were men—rarely arrived on time. I, on the other hand, couldn't afford to be late. I couldn't miss my terribly important appointment at high noon on May 12.

Unlike the run-up to my departure from California four years earlier, I couldn't sleep those last nights before setting sail. I was exhausted as well from parties, last-minute television appearances, and radio and newspaper interviews. I was trying to show the appearance of a worldly woman soon off to sea. On the Wednesday before departure, I hosted a dinner for the navy friends who had helped me secure provisions and load the boat. Another day, Mayor Asukata Ichio threw a luncheon at the New Grand Hotel. And yet another party had been organized by the U.S. Consulate in its gardens, with two hundred engraved invitations mailed to the biggest dignitaries in the city. Ladies in kimonos, men in formal suits. The gardens were dressed in pink of every shade, with rhododendrons and azaleas in full bloom. My six-thousand-mile sail to San Diego was to be but a small tribute from Yokohama to San Diego in honor of the city's two-hundredth-anniversary celebrations.

On Saturday, May 10, I invited my navy friends to accompany me while I took *Sea Sharp II* to Yokohama two days before our scheduled departure. I couldn't show off the wind vane since I didn't know how to use it, so instead I just let each person take turns steering. They were delighted with the opportunity, and I successfully hid my deficiency.

We anchored in front of the New Grand Hotel's friendship garden, which was given to the people of Yokohama from the people of San Diego. Hands across the ocean. A large concrete "goddess of the sea" faces San Diego from a small pond in a glorious setting.

My last day ashore, I had a long, hot shower and shampoo in an actual bathroom with fresh running water. Tony Bennett was singing that night at the officer's club, and though I was invited to see him, I couldn't possibly attend. I couldn't stop crying and throwing up. Fear and anxiety were catching up with me.

The morning of May 12, 1969, arrived soon enough, and I couldn't avoid departure day. I didn't even look at the weather at 6:00 a.m.; I just plowed ahead with the day, my gut in a tizzy. It had been ten months since I concocted this brilliant idea and presented it to Clair in a Long Beach coffee shop. Ten months, perhaps not long enough.

Help greeted me at the dock: butane for the stove, water for the tanks, and a big plastic tub for storing my cameras. But I had plenty more to worry about. The wind vane still didn't work. Carpenters were still tinkering on the boat. Canon had brought me six 8 mm cameras, which needed to be stored. Plus, the stays and shrouds needed some final tuning.

Japanese customs officers didn't know what to do with me. Of course, Clair was there to see me off, so he was a big help with officials. How would they get me out of the country? They'd never dealt with such a case before. There were many harried looks when the officials saw my crew list of one, a woman at that. The boat didn't even belong to me; it belonged to Clair, which complicated matters further. Finally, they had me sign a heap of papers as though *Sea Sharp II* had been an ocean liner. I signed everything as "master of the vessel."

Come midmorning, I looked at the weather report, which I received in daily installments from the U.S. Navy weather bureau in

Yokosuka. It was a beautiful day with a few puffy clouds, nothing like the pelting rain the day before when a CBS crew had shown up for an interview. The weather bureau predicted blue skies for my departure, but those favorable conditions wouldn't see me much beyond the bay. Gale-force winds raged 250 miles out, and I was sure to hit them.

"Maybe my first, but not my last," I told myself. "I'll have to face them."

I entered the throngs of people gathered at the docks. I was dressed in a pink and white pantsuit, to match the pink on *Sea Sharp II*. A delegation from the mayor's office had arrived to give me two letters for personal delivery to the mayors of Los Angeles and San Diego. A representative from Citizen Watch Company, which had supplied me with a watch, dressed me in a pink and white lei. In those days, of course, the company could offer me a watch but not yet their mobile Internet devices, LED lamps, or electronic health gadgets that sailors would come to rely on, thirty-five years later.

Mr. Sato, the boatyard foreman stood on deck, shaking his head. "No trouble, no trouble," was all he said. I'm not fully sure what he meant, but I took it as his wish for fair winds.

The usual suspects had gathered on the dock: AP, UPI, CBS, Reuters, and a pod of Japanese journalists. So many, yet they all had the same question: "How do you feel right now?" They all wanted to know if I was scared. "Terrified!" I cried, so they all got the pictures their editors wanted of the woman so many people presumed would never return.

But the onlookers were soon drowned out by chanting children, hundreds of them dressed in blue jackets and yellow beanies, shouting in unison, "Goodbye Mrs. Adams!" They lined the deck of the *Hikawa Maru*, a 331-passenger liner that had been turned into a ship of all trades—hotel, restaurant, museum, and convention center. In her day, the *Hikawa Maru* was known as the Queen of the Pacific, until she was converted into a hospital ship during World War II. That day, the ship was a reviewing platform for all those school kids.

Several Japanese women in the crowd pressed small gifts into my hands. One sixteen-year-old girl, who had traveled hours by train to see me, handed me a small, egg-shaped stuffed head covered in pink yarn, a gift from her grandmother. The head had only one eye; such was an old Japanese custom. When a family member embarked on a long expedition, that eye was to see only safety for the journey. Upon the voyager's safe arrival, he—or she—was to add the other eye to the head. I was so touched; I would look at it often throughout the trip and vowed to paint the other eye when I reached home.

At 11:00 a.m. the Yokohama city firemen's band arrived and began its medley of tunes with "John Brown's Body" perhaps better known as "The Battle Hymn of the Republic," with its ominous line about the poor corpse "a-mouldering in the grave." Oh, those kindly Japanese—they had no idea the words they played.

But when the clock hit noon, the firemen's band switched its tune and belted out "Anchors Aweigh." *Sea Sharp II*'s sails were raised and luffing; I trimmed them and crept away from the dock. There were so many people, so many well wishes, so much noise. I was so nervous, so emotional, I don't even recall casting off the last line.

But I wasn't alone yet; the crowd felt familiar. The U.S. Navy captain's gig followed me, and so did a couple of press boats with photographers, who kept clicking as long and far as they could through Tokyo Bay. I couldn't think about them. I concentrated on the task at hand, which was to get around all those ships before I hit the outer Yokohama breakwater. Then it was another twenty miles before reaching the neck of the bay. All that before dark. The commotion faded behind me, but I looked ahead.

The sky was clear; the water, calm; and the boat felt like she'd been at sea for ages. That was good. After an hour, I reached for a brown-bag lunch that a lady had handed me. She had packed a roast-beef sandwich, carrot sticks, and fresh strawberries. I would have nothing so enticing for weeks to come. I ate, and then, when no one was there to watch me, I removed my pink pantsuit, put on sweatshirt and jeans, and packed my sailing suit for as long as it would take.

By midafternoon *Sea Sharp II* and I were fifteen miles down the bay, and the navy boat turned back toward its base. The photographers took their last pictures, and we waved our good-byes. I watched behind me as they blended into the horizon. Now I was alone, truly alone.

What lay ahead was the world's biggest ocean, more than sixty million square miles of liquid, larger than all the earth's landmasses put together. It's been called the angry ocean, in defiance of its name. The currents at the opening of Tokyo Bay were sometimes violent, sometimes rough, I had been told. But we passed through with little ado, and I gave myself a mental pat on the back. There we were in the North Pacific, just the boat and her captain in the unknown.

No time for relaxing. Lots of traffic was heading in and out of Tokyo Bay, and I didn't want to be caught anywhere near the entrance by nightfall. I could still see bits of land, but not for long. Shortly after dark, I stared at the Nojima Saki lighthouse, the last land light I would see for weeks. I looked until I could see light no more.

I couldn't attempt to let the boat self-steer until I was free of the shipping lanes, so I had to stick by the wheel. It was dark and quiet, just the slip-slap of nighttime water against the boat. But I couldn't unwind, not after the hectic weeks I'd had. I still wasn't sure of the boat, the wind vane, or myself.

There's no defying nature though. By 1:00 a.m., I could do no more. I kept the running lights and spreader lights burning, still wary of traffic just offshore. Then, I brought my sleeping bag into the cockpit to attempt a few catnaps as *Sea Sharp II* tried her best to steer the right course.

Alone Again on Water

May 13. Thirty hours and twenty minutes since we left Yokohama, it was foggy and rainy all day with winds at twenty-eight to thirty miles per hour—from the wrong direction. *Sea Sharp II* rode along most easily at a close reach on a heading of 150 degrees, but since she couldn't sail herself, it was up to me. By watching what was happening just as she would start to veer off course, I finally figured I needed to balance all the sails with the helm's rudder before engaging the clutch of the vane, rather than the other way around as I had been told. The vane had its own small rudder, which couldn't overcome the power of *Sea Sharp II*'s sails as well as the larger rudder. It took several hours of experimenting, but I finally had the answer.

We suffered the normal creaking of a boat at work, plus a few cans rattling around in stowage. The stove groaned, but I didn't know why. Not too much had shifted, despite the winds and waves. We had water over the starboard decks, three waves in the cockpit, and one over the cabin top; *Sea Sharp II* took it all like a lady, keeping her course. We weren't making much headway, but I was proud of the boat's performance. We were still getting to know each other. She did great; she did better than I.

I wasn't keeping anything down. Every bite I ate came up again, in vicious ways. I was sure it was anxiety, fear, and exhaustion. I ate soda crackers and drank ginger ale. Nothing worked, but anything coming up was better than dry heaves. Already I was counting the days, seventy-nine more to reach San Diego. Seventy-nine days! How could I start counting so soon—that would surely drive me into a fit of misery. All I could do was sleep and hope for a better tomorrow.

Every day at sea, I talked to my tape recorder. It became my companion, my confidant. To the little machine, I bared my thoughts and feelings. It was my diary, my record of life. I felt like the world could listen—but of course it could not. I knew that; I had been through this before. Yet I kept talking, kept recording. Perhaps that's what maintained my sanity.

May 14. I awoke at 4:00 a.m. for no reason. We had wandered slightly off course, so I put on my foul-weather gear and headed out to retrim the wind vane. A faint pink colored the foggy morning sky. Then suddenly, a three-masted square-rigger appeared out of the eerie fog like a scene from a B-rate horror flick. It was a Japanese training ship sailing to San Diego, just as I was, for the city's bicentennial celebrations. The square-rigger had been heading east but changed her course to approach my side. She had a crew of 143 young Japanese seamen, and I swear each one of them lined her rails, waving, wishing me luck. They knew who I was, and they saluted with two long blasts of the whistle before vanishing into the ghostly white air. Fog swallowed her masts and rigging, then erased her wake, too.

That afternoon, the winds dropped and the seas calmed; by night, I could see stars. I finally downed my first hot meal of chicken and noodles, finishing with a candy bar. The air felt pleasant. Still, heavy clouds hung in the northeast sky, and I thought of rain for the next day. Weather was the most important fixture of the day. For one thing: I had to live with it. For another: it was the single feature that had the power to get us home.

May 15. I flew out of my sleeping bag at 4:30 a.m. to a terrible noise, a crack like a gunshot. I raced to the deck and found the genoa dragging over the side. The halyard cable had split, blown apart, and the sail whipped around like a wild dragon as I hauled it on board.

The seas were beginning to build again, eight to ten feet. There was no time to fix the broken halyard. I had to spend all my energy keeping on course. With the staysail and mizzen, we were doing only two knots. My God, I couldn't bear to think how long it would take to reach San Diego at that rate. We wouldn't make it. Three days into a transpacific crossing, and a portion of brand-new cable—something checked and rechecked and checked again—had mysteriously snapped. How could that be? It looked to be cut clean about halfway through before the other strands exploded, curling out and down like flower petals bursting forth.

May 16. The nausea had passed, but I continued to throw up periodically. So much for optimism.

That morning at 3:00, I awoke depressed. I decided to read Kenichi Horie's *Kodoku: Sailing Alone Across the Pacific*. In 1962 he had been the first Japanese to single-hand the giant ocean, at the age of twenty-three. He also had departed on May 12. I felt we had some kind of connection. It took him ninety-four days. What did he feel like in the first stretch of his voyage? I wanted to know.

I discovered his first two weeks were the worst. It was encouraging—sad for him but good for me. The winds blew Horie the wrong way; he didn't move. Then a typhoon struck him, poor guy. For my sake, I felt better reading that. I hadn't had a gale, and *Sea Sharp II* was a more comfortable boat. Horie had had only nineteen feet; *Sea Sharp II* offered twelve feet beyond that. In fact, I had everything I needed but strength. It was my stomach that threatened to sink us.

My wind changed at 7:00 a.m., coming from the east-southeast. I had to tack and raise more sail so we could get on the move. I needed the genoa back up for the added speed, but the emergency halyard was made of the same cable that had broken. Would it last? For eleven weeks? I had to try. It was a two-hour struggle to raise that sail again, to untangle the genny and sheets from the clump I had dumped them in the previous day. The job exhausted me.

After a short rest, I raised the main, and we started to skim along at a respectable speed over moderate seas. My only thought of food at that moment was the dinner I had enjoyed with my friends Larry and Yvette before leaving; I dreamed of a fresh strawberry Bavarian dessert with champagne. . . . "Next Wednesday night, I'll be at sea thinking of this lovely evening," I had told them. Boy, was I right.

Well, that Wednesday, three days out, I hadn't eaten much; but carefully stowed beneath the dinette table, I had a big tin box that Yvette had given to me on departure day. She had called it my "Wednesday Box," stuffed with homemade brandy balls, pecan pie, and eight kinds of assorted treats. That box could get me through anything! My salvage, my safety.

I must confess I had thoughts of turning back, even as early as day five. When I was sick, when the halyard broke, I didn't want to go on. Nor could I turn back to Japan. I couldn't have faced my friends or the wonderful people who put so much love, so much sweat, into building that boat. Nor could I face the world. I simply couldn't have lived with myself. Thousands of people had seen me leave Tokyo Bay. Most were strangers, of course, but I somehow felt obliged to please them. When I thought of all that, I grew determined that the world would see me again in San Diego.

Later in the day, the sun came out for an hour and dried the boat. The morning mist had removed some of the salt from the previous days of crashing waves. The sea was calm, but the barometer had fallen. Did that mean an oncoming squall or steady rain? We just sat there, going nowhere, but at least we were pointed in the right direction.

I took advantage of the smooth water. I swept the cabin carpet, cleaned the stove, washed my hair, and filed my nails real short. That was the extent of my housekeeping. Then, I put on my handywoman's hat and tried to fix all the little things I had intended to address later, like the broken shock cord on the port fairlead block. I stood on the winch handle in an attempt to hoist the genny a few more inches, but that didn't really work. What else could I do? I only weighed around 115 pounds. Some jobs I perpetually left for later.

We made ten miles that afternoon at full sail. I wasn't going to hope for greater winds, though. I was sure I would have regretted such a wish as soon as the next big storm hit.

Meanwhile, this trip I came prepared. I brought books, lots of books, and already I had finished one. I brought reading for every mood: Athol Thomas's *Forgotten Eden: A View of the Seychelles Islands in the Indian Ocean*; Samuel Eliot Morison's *Admiral of the Ocean Sea: A Life of Christopher Columbus*; Charles Borden's *Sea Quest*; Art Linkletter's *Linkletter Down Under*; and *Uhuru*, a story of freedom in Kenya by Robert Ruark. And I had a Bible. Just before I left Los Angeles, my reverend handed me the bright red book. He actually apologized for the color. "I'm sorry I couldn't find a pink one for you."

Those who came to my launch also had doled out presents to me at the dock. There were many, but I'd opened only the biggest at that point in my voyage. It was a Japanese doll in a glass case, eighteen by eleven by nine inches, with real human hair and a brocade kimono. I securely fastened her in the forepeak to protect against breakage.

As for my attire, the temperature was sixty degrees at least, not too cold, so I was comfortable in a sweatshirt, jeans, and heavy socks. I didn't wear shoes but slipped into sea boots whenever I went on deck. Sometimes I wore furry Peruvian alpaca slippers in the cabin.

May 17. I awoke in the dark again, 4:00 a.m., which quickly became an unintended habit. The wind had swung in from the south, and when I went out on deck, a beautiful white tern was perched on a stanchion. When I let the mainsail out, the bird flew in a circle then settled again on the lifeline beside me. I talked to it. I told it I was sorry there wasn't enough light because I wasn't sure the picture I had taken of it would turn out. I asked the tern to stay, for I enjoyed its company. But it soon flew away.

The wind had risen steadily all morning, and we made five knots. *Sea Sharp II* occasionally got knocked around, but we always came back on track. I guess I'd finally made friends with the wind vane. It was like a spoiled child. Every time I went on deck to spank the thing back into order, it settled down and behaved.

But by noon nothing sounded right. Nothing felt right. It was intuition. I knew it was time to shorten sail. I knew the louvers on the top fashion board—in layman's terms, the front of the cabin, something like a door that could be stowed below—should have been covered in plastic to keep water out. Within a few hours, we'd hit winds roaring at forty miles per hour. Suddenly—WHOMP! Gusts and bigger gusts. I managed to get the mainsail down and furled. The anemometer read winds at forty-four miles per hour. I had hit the predicted gale.

I took the first seas into the cockpit. The boat was sealed as best as she could be; we would handle green water without much consequence. I didn't have much sail up, but because we held at four knots on good course, I decided to ride with it.

Then a wave broadsided us and kicked the wind out of the sails. More green water rushed into the cockpit. I was thoroughly drenched and went back inside for dry clothes. The wind had increased only slightly, but the seas were building. *Sea Sharp II* couldn't keep her course; we were battered from side to side, rolling with the blows, trying to stay upright.

We learn by doing, I kept thinking. But that wasn't much comfort against such seas. I didn't know what to do. Was half the staysail too much? Should I raise the storm trysail? For a while, I couldn't open the hatch; one wave after another crashed over the top. Even a small, six-foot wave was too high.

I would talk myself through it. I would keep yammering into my recorder until a solution came through. Maybe I could outtalk, outwit, outthink the storm. Thank God for Plexiglas, or I wouldn't have had any windows left.

It was a greenish gray scud that pummeled us on all sides, coming from the tops of the waves. Thankfully, *Sea Sharp II* seemed to dance to the gyrations of the seas, showing no signs of real distress.

I had to go outside. I had to furl the staysail a little more. I sat out there, watching the waves build behind us, watching the wind vane vibrate. WHOOSH. Water filled the cockpit and sent all the lines swimming like spaghetti in a bowl of water. I dashed inside for yet another set of clothes.

"It could be much worse," I told myself. All was secure. I was well. I was warm and dry. The boat was dry inside. All I had to do was crawl over and switch on the running lights so I could see. No need for kerosene amid a squall. Nope, I'd stay right there, snug in my bunk with a book in hand.

So I thought.

I'd padded my bed with extra cushions, but they weren't enough to counteract the constant rolling. I thought of my fear as I sailed to Hawaii. Oh, what I hadn't known then!

I swore I wouldn't go outside again, but through the dome, I could see that one of the running backstays on the main mast had slipped. No way could I sleep without the boat taken care of to the best of my ability.

I reached into my Wednesday Box for a brandy ball. And I braved the elements once more on deck. Even fully wrapped in foul-weather gear, I was soaked inside. The water rushed up my sleeve and gushed down my back every time I raised my arms. If that happened again, I would have had no more dry clothes.

May 18. I must have slept. I'm not sure what held us through the night, but when I awoke, I could see nothing through the dome. Zero visibility. We rode the sea like a rollercoaster, *Sea Sharp II* with her nose sky high, then into the troughs as the waves rolled beneath us.

I'd try to move, only to be slammed against the boat, bruised and battered. Try going to the bathroom like that. I had to hang on with both hands, and a woman needs at least one hand free to get her pants down and up again.

We crashed on a wave so big it lifted the lid off the icebox, flung it across the room, and left a nasty nick in the varnish. How long could this last? I had heard these storms could rage for many hours—but could I?

I was on hands and knees in front of the galley when I felt water. It was over the floorboards. Where had it come from? I knew I had pumped the bilge the night before and it was dry. But now, what a mess. It took me an hour to get the jerricans of fresh water out of the bilge compartment. I started scooping the gunk with a bucket and pouring it overboard. But it wasn't only water down there. There was oil down there, too—the remnants of an oil change before my departure. My arms sank into a slimy cesspool of water and crud. What I found was a handful of wet sawdust and wood shavings plugging the holes that enabled water to drain to the lowest point where it could be drained by the bilge pumps. I don't know how all that gunk got in there.

But now I had wet, smelly carpet.

And I had wet, smelly me.

I had cleaned the bilge before leaving; it had been spotless. I wanted to scream. Yes, I could scream, but no one would hear me. Like a tree falling in the woods—the sound of my anger would leave no impression on anyone.

By evening *Sea Sharp II* steered herself. She was a far more skillful skipper than I could have been. She had no emotion. She faced that storm without anger or sadness, without question or despair. But damage was done. A five-gallon water can had broken free; the starboard radar reflector had disappeared.

Sea stories are funny things. There are tall tales and suspect accounts. A sailor rarely has proof, like the fisherman and the fish that got away. But a sailor doesn't lie to her logbook. It wouldn't make sense. The logbook is the sailor's only point of dead reckoning, and she can't make that up. So that day, I recorded a record 99.75 miles in less than twenty-four hours, with not even half a staysail. That's how strong the wind was, how forceful the sea. That's the yang of a stormy yin.

I just prayed for no more broken parts; I couldn't face the weather and the journey with a broken boat. "The first two weeks will be the hardest," Clair had told me. "The first four hundred miles." Well, by the end of week one, we had logged 408 miles in a storm.

May 19. The wind let up a bit, and I started to reassemble the boat. I coiled the lines, greased the wind vane bearings, ran the engine, charged the batteries, and pumped the bilge—all dry.

I hadn't slept at all that night, not with pelting rain. *Sea Sharp II* was dry inside, but my foul-weather gear dripped all over the cabin, my clothes were muggy, and my sleeping bag stank of the damp.

I was so tired my memory stopped working. I wouldn't remember the day unless I crossed it off the calendar. I couldn't think straight either; I couldn't think pleasant thoughts. I thought of torture chambers, of dizzying rotating rooms—how long could a human being last?

May 20. I dipped into serious depression for the first time. Only eight days out, and I was soaked through my pores, with a heap of dirty laundry. I lived in a one-piece padded coverall, confined to a little cramp of a cabin. Solitary confinement. A mental abyss.

May 21. There was a stubborn wind again at 4:00 a.m. I set the foreguys, afterguys, boom vang, preventers, and running backstays just in time for the wind to switch ninety degrees. So I tacked and did it all again. Can the master wind cackle at its human slave?

By noon we moved steadily through a downpour, and I began to clean. I scoured the galley, swept the carpet, and hung my disgusting clothes in the cleansing rain. I put a bucket beneath the main boom and collected some of the fresh rainwater coming off the sail. It didn't take long before I had collected enough for a bath. I put the bucket in the cockpit, and as I trimmed sails, we hit a big wave. Over went the bucket.

So I started again. I filled another bucket, heated some of the water on the stove, and prepared for a warm bath; but the wind veered again. On with the foul-weather gear once more. When I came in from outside an hour later, my bathwater had, of course, gone cold.

May 22. I changed the clocks, one hour ahead. It was psychological. Somehow it felt better to read 5:00 a.m. instead of 4:00 a.m. when I awoke to an inevitably onerous day.

But that morning started with blue sky, sun, and seventy degrees. I tore the boat apart: laundry hung from every hook and line. Pillow, sleeping bag, boots, rain gear, rags, clothes—everything was airing out in the sun.

I worked on navigation and discovered we had drifted only thirty miles off course. Not bad, I thought, after ten days and a gale. My log read 635 miles behind us, not far off the goal I had made of ten degrees of longitude per week.

But it was daunting to look at my progress. The Pacific is too big to fit onto one chart; right then, I saw Japan on the left and nothing on the right—just the big, empty ocean. It was as though I sailed toward the edge of the world, where I would disappear from the paper. I folded my chart into thirds just so I couldn't see the edge. Just so I could hope.

TWELVE

Things Fall Apart

May 23. I awoke at 7:00 a.m. The wind had swung around from the east and pointed us south. I decided to eat breakfast before tacking; otherwise I'd forget. I always forgot to eat when things got busy.

Half an hour later, while still eating breakfast, the staysail fell over the side, furled. Just like that, it was under the boat and scraping the bottom. Since it was still furled, I was able to bring it back on board without as much trouble as I had had with the genny. When I took a look, I discovered the problem—not the halyard that time but the halyard block itself.

Only seven hundred miles, and both headsails were inoperable. What next?

Before anything else, I had to climb the mast to replace the staysail block. I slugged some coffee and thought the problem through. I would have to take both the staysail and halyard blocks apart to get the halyard in the new halyard block. The wind was picking up; the seas were growing choppy. It is one thing to take yourself up a mast in your peaceful dock at home, and it is quite another when the top of the mast has a thirty- to forty-degree swing. When I got up there, I had one foot on the top rung of the ladder, the other leg wrapped around the shrouds, one arm over the spreader, and the other free to maneuver. My pockets were full of tools but no wire cutters. I couldn't get the shackle to budge.

So I descended, trimmed the sails for a smoother run, and scrambled up the mast again with wire cutters. The shackle had wedged itself together, and there was no way on God's blue sea I could get it to open. I tried using my pliers handle to pry it; the handle bent. I could put another shackle up there, but then the halyard would lead incorrectly. I'd need three shackles for it to work correctly, but I didn't have a third spare that same size.

Down I went again, dripping blood all the way. I had clung so hard to the shroud up there that it had torn straight through the flesh of my hand. I disinfected the wound, bound my hand, and left the staysail for another time.

The truth is I felt sorry for myself. The entire day, I wanted to curl up and cry. I ached all over, my hand still stung, my leg was covered in bruises. It hurt to walk, it hurt to sit, and the underside of my arm swelled like a pickle.

What's more, a black cloud hovered over us, turning everything in my world dark. Lightning shot from turbulent skies. I had no desire to move. I wanted to hunker below and let *Sea Sharp II* guide us through the night. But that wouldn't do. I had to take the mainsail down; the wind was blowing more than thirty-five miles per hour. What a bad sailor. I had thought of myself before my boat.

Just a few good days, that's all I wanted. Then I could catch up—I could repair the broken parts and work on maintenance. So many things needed fixing—the sliding hatch, the mizzen-running backstay, the main winch. They all had problems.

May 24. By then, I'd learned this much: there's no use in wiping yourself out when you're single-handing. You have no helping hands, and it doesn't matter if you arrive behind schedule so long as you eventually arrive. If you work too hard, you won't make it at all. So on May 24, I did nothing but rest.

May 25. I learned we had sailed 110 miles on my day off. I'd had little to do with it.

I reached a point where I hated going on deck, hated what I might find. Next time I went topside, it was the main topping lift, which I found in two pieces over the side. How could that have happened? The cable was shot, blown, ripped apart two feet from where it crossed over the fitting at the masthead. There had been no strain on it. I'd used it only when raising or lowering the mainsail. It should not have broken. Did someone have it in for me? Maybe I wasn't meant to get home?

I ate quickly and set to work again, fixing yet more broken parts. The wind grew as the day wore on, and I knew I would have to control that boom somehow while getting it down for repairs without it swinging over and breaking my bubble. I tried lowering it just a few inches, hoping it would hold in the boom crutch. That didn't work, but I had sore muscles to show for the effort. I laid the boom on the cabin top, hoping we wouldn't heel before I secured it. To this day, I don't know how I lifted that eighty-four-pound boom as high as my shoulders up into the crutch, but I got the job done. I wore a glove all day, but my hand still bled straight through.

At 8:00 p.m. the weather turned again; the seas whipped into a froth as the winds brewed. I'd become intensely aware of noises; every new creak or rattle, gurgle or moan sent me searching for a source. I'd usually find my vitamins shaking in their bottle, or a pencil rolling back and forth. But I had to know. I'd become a fraidy cat with keen ears that could discern tiny hums and burbles over the howling wind and rain.

May 26. In the morning, I was back to repairing. I used my hand drill and screws to secure a block on the forward side of the mizzen mast, as high as I could reach. Then I jury-rigged a fitting on the end of the boom to hook into the block. The rest of the way home, this meant two trips back and forth on deck to the halyard winch each time I raised or lowered the sail. It was the best I could do, and it worked for me.

Another one thousand miles, and we'd be due north of Midway. That would put us 2,800 miles from San Francisco and 2,200 miles from Japan. Midway was the atoll made famous in World War II when the Americans handed the Japanese a pivotal defeat. I told myself if we had suffered more major breakage by then, I could sail south and go in for repairs, even though I didn't have a chart. Midway would be my point of reckoning. It had turned the war around; it might turn me, as well.

We passed through another heavy blow during the previous night but I was out only once to furl half the staysail. What a beautiful but eerie sea, alight with phosphorescence in green waters that tampered with the imagination. It furled and crested; it was like sailing through a sea of sparklers on the Fourth of July.

Two weeks at sea were crossed off the calendar. We had sailed 914 miles by noon that day. I hoped to cross the international date line by the end of five weeks. I had the feeling we were sailing uphill to the international date line, all downhill after that. Crazy, of course. The sea is flat, but the mind sees life the way it wants to.

May 27. People think a sailor leads a life of adventure and discovery. However, those moments come in blips, in between the humdrum. Therefore, a second straight day of good sailing, to me, meant a chance to catch up on maintenance. I spent that morning taking apart the main halyard winch and greasing it, putting another shackle up the mast, getting the staysail up, replacing broken shock cord, oiling the blocks and turnbuckles, and airing out my sleeping bag. In all that, I discovered the cotter keys were missing from three lifeline turnbuckles—which says I hadn't been doing very good inspections. Had I not found the problem, I easily could have slipped into a watery grave, unable to pull myself back on board.

May 28. I started cutting the material for a dress, bright pink with white lace trim; it was something to occupy the time and keep my fingers busy. I had planned to sew, and I packed accordingly. I sprayed the scissors with WD-40 and packed them in plastic, along with my needles and pins. I sewed by hand, happy as a lark under the warmth of the bubble.

That afternoon, I finished the last piece of pecan pie from my Wednesday Box. And by that evening, I felt a deep pit of loneliness. That happened from time to time, without warning or reason, just dark moments of despair. And it made no sense, as we'd had a good day, moving steadily at five knots. Maybe the constant rolling and pitching has a cumulative effect on the psyche; it just gnaws at the body and mind. "Please hold still, just for five minutes," I prayed. I wanted to get off the boat or to go to bed and bury my head. I wanted to yelp. What the hell was I doing?

I tried to talk to myself—that didn't work. I tried to walk around the deck—what an absurd idea. I listened to the radio, but that didn't improve my mood. I tried a crossword puzzle, but it was no use. So I drank two glasses of wine and went to bed by 9:00 p.m.

May 29. My thirty-ninth birthday.

Happy birthday, hell! I had vowed to bake a cake and wear some pretty clothes; I would open the presents I had stowed and treat myself to a birthday party of one. But the silence woke me at 2:30 a.m. The wind had died, and we sat in the idle sea. I went outside and strapped in the sails to cut down the slatting. I returned to bed.

By 6:00 a.m., we had started to move. I made coffee and opened a can of stewed prunes. When the wind died, I had learned, it meant we would change directions—and it did. Two steady days of northwest air suddenly switched to coming from the southeast. I had to tack, so I took the pole down from the genny, secured it on deck, and returned to the cockpit. I turned the helm to change course, and just as we came about, down came the genny. Over the side again, trailing in the water. I swore up, down, and all around, words unfit for print, words I barely knew I had within me! I had ordered the best cable I could find and had it sent to Japan, just to prevent this sort of disaster! There had to be a reason all this was happening.

It took two hours to rope and tie the sail, like wrestling with a wild steer. Inch by inch, I tugged it in while leaning over the side. Just as I pulled in the last few inches, a gust of wind picked it up and tossed the sail over the side again, nearly taking me with it. My arms felt heavy like lead. I started over, desperately trying to rescue the sail, to rescue me.

Once the sail was lashed to the deck, secured to the stanchions with gaskets, I sat for a moment of reflection. This was my birthday, and I spent it thinking about all that breakage. What had I done wrong? To whom? Why me?

By noon I decided that since it was, after all, my birthday and I had promised myself that Betty Crocker and I would have a date. We would make a cake. It came in a box, though I didn't have an egg to make good batter. Nor was it worth the propane to heat the oven to bake it. So I put the batter in my frying pan on top of the stove. No frosting either, but I stuck six candles into the blob, lit them, and stuck my fingers into the middle, just like a little kid. I even set up a camera to record the festivities. I tried to smile and look happy, really. Then I opened a present: a carved silver ring that matched a little bell I had been wearing around my neck since the day before I left for Hawaii, four years earlier.

With that done, I tossed the remaining cake overboard. Too

messy, totally unfit to eat. Maybe the gooney birds could celebrate for me.

It was a black, black night with another squall on the horizon. I settled down to the news: Mayor Sam Yorty had won reelection in Los Angeles. Hearing his name made me think of the letter I delivered to him four years earlier on my first crossing.

I'd been writing my own letters to new friends in Japan, pages and pages long, every day a new addendum, which turned them into sagas from the sea. The letters kept me busy.

I went to bed that night with a book in hand and prayers on my mind for all those friends who remembered me, all the people who kept me in their own prayers. So far away they were, yet we all looked up to the same night sky.

May 30. Memorial Day, the day we commemorate those lost in war. Coincidentally, I spent it thinking about putting in at Midway. Of course I found more amiss that morning. I found the mizzen topping lift down, cut straight through the cable, sharp and smooth, as though sliced by wire cutters. How? Had we been issued a bad reel of cable? Were the blocks faulty? I would never learn the answer. I could overcome the problem; the mizzen sail and boom were smaller and still manageable without a topping lift. But I worried about "what else." What else would break? What else could possibly go wrong? Nearly every day, it was something. Soon I would reach the point of no return; no choice but to turn toward Midway. We hadn't even sailed a third of the way; 4,700 miles remained. I would sail to the date line and make my decision then.

That afternoon, I checked the taffrail log and took a reading of our position. It wasn't turning. I pulled it up from the water and found two-thirds of the line and the rotator were gone. Simply gone. That rotator had trailed my wake for seven thousand miles, and now it had disappeared. It must have been one monster shark, to have swallowed an eight-inch metal rotator with three fins. Hope he had a grumpy gut! Thank goodness I had a spare.

I dreamt in fits that night, nightmares about broken parts and pirates aboard the boat, strange things afoot in the middle of the Pacific.

And then I awoke to calm seas and skies, for an entire day and a half.

June 1. A new month, a new week, a new page on my calendar. A smooth sky and friendly seas welcomed me; I finally started to feel better. I washed my hair that morning and rinsed some panties in leftover rainwater. I took stock of body and mind: I felt strong, despite having lost considerable weight. My hand lesions were healing and no longer looked like bloody raw claws. My bruises had improved and turned into intriguing shades of chartreuse. All was well.

And then.

And then the winds blew and blew; the sky sank dark upon us long before its normal course. It rained again, and I pulled back the hatch to check the anemometer. Just then, a wave smacked the cabin so hard it forced me to duck. I cracked my forehead on the top fashion board, stunning myself into a stupor. I fell and landed on my funny bone while water gushed through the open hatchway. Not only was I bruised and stymied, I had soaked myself and ruined my fresh shampoo.

And then.

And then another wave came while I was in the head. I braced myself against the door, but it wasn't securely fastened. The force of the sea flung me out of the head and through the cabin with my pants around my ankles. What a sight! I'm glad I'm the only one who saw it. I managed to land on the bunk—not a very stylish move, but my butt emerged unscathed.

It took two hours to secure all of the sails and put up a reefed heavy-storm trysail. I have never been totally without sail. I didn't feel right without some stability for *Sea Sharp II* to be able to steer. What I had up wasn't much, but it was something.

By 10:30 p.m., I knew I was in for a sleepless night. It was a sou'easter we faced. I'd never seen the ocean build like that, an inferno of roiling water. Towering walls of sea. Wind screaming through the rigging. The barometer pressure was falling rapidly. I was all decked out in foul-weather gear with a towel around my neck and rubber bands on my wrists and ankles to keep the water out—but it was to no avail since I was soaked like a sponge. I shouldn't have looked around. When we hit the bottom of a trough, water towered like liquid mountains ready to collapse upon us. Then up we'd go back up as though cresting a roller coaster that would suddenly collapse beneath us. It rained so hard I couldn't see past the bow of the boat. While I was in the cockpit adjusting the wind vane, my gallon bucket filled with rainwater in minutes despite the rain's horizontal blowing. Inside, I padded myself in a bunker of foam-rubber cushions from the dinette. It was a trying night; I would doze a few winks but awaken every time the sea shook us. This went on throughout the night; I stayed in bed until noon, riding the storm out. There was nothing else to do.

June 3. Storm was on the way out, spotty clouds and sun were on the way in. I had survived. I inspected the deck and found nothing else broken or missing, just a burned-out starboard running light, which I had noticed in the storm. It shouldn't matter; I had the kerosene lights as back-up. Another ordeal come and gone and chalked to success.

What, though, would I do about all those scratches, all those nicks in the finish, all those marks that advertised my misadventures at sea? It wasn't my boat after all. I couldn't deliver a wreck.

So I set to cleaning up. I greased the wind vane. I covered the deck in wet clothes, towels, rags, cushions, carpets, and pillows, all set to dry in the approaching sun. I'd been through that routine before, every time it stormed.

As I worked, a small squid came aboard as though to say hi; I gently helped him back in the water, toward his friends. He swam away, and on the horizon a rainbow stretched from end to end.

Really, it did.

THIRTEEN

74 Days, 17 Hours, 15 Minutes

June 4. As usual, I was flustered. I was completely rattled, shaken, knocked out of my element. I awoke at 4:30 that morning to scan the horizon and check the rigging and compass course before returning to bed. An hour and a half later I was rudely awakened by the loudest whistle blast I shall ever hear. It scared me beyond words. When I looked up through the window, I saw the big black bow of the American President Lines SS *President McKinley*. She was a twelve-passenger, seven-hatch freighter, and she was slowly approaching our lee side.

I shot out of my sleeping bag like a cannon ball, reached to fling open the hatch, and remembered I was naked. Let me tell you, there's no easy trick to putting damp clothes onto dry skin while clinging to a rocking boat. Nor is there an easy way to put on sweat pants using one hand when one of the legs is turned inside out. As I wrestled with my obstinate clothing, the *McKinley* blew repeated blasts, longer and louder. "Where are you?" it seemed to shout.

I was crying alligator tears, trembling all over, screaming, "I'm coming, I'm coming."

Flashbulbs were popping as I emerged on deck.

"Are you all right?" the captain asked.

"Yes." I was so stunned, that's all I could say.

"Is there anything you need?"

I took a long pause before answering. "No." There were so many things I wanted—a cheese sandwich, for instance—but that wasn't his question.

"Your position is 35°59'N, 172°2'E."

It was hard to hear over the distance and wind, but I caught enough to know I was just fine. "Thank you," I said. And that was it. The captain told me he'd report the sighting to the home office and tell them I was OK. "It was nice seeing you," he said nonchalantly with a big wave. Then the ship was gone. It was over the horizon so fast; there I was alone—again.

Such excitement, I barely took pictures. I just couldn't think straight. It was such an unexpected visit that I didn't know what to say or do. It was the first encounter, the first conversation, I'd had in twenty-two days. Twenty-two days, and all I'd said was "Yes. . . . No. . . . Thank you." Some socialite I was! Had solitary confinement stolen my ability to think in the presence of other humans? My life at sea didn't include visitors, and the whole ordeal—all three minutes of it—threw my mind off kilter. The *McKinley* represented a world from which I had divorced myself, at least temporarily. The people on board had disrupted my life. I'm sure they had no such intentions; I'm sure they had no idea they'd done it. But a simple occurrence like the quick appearance of a ship and the brief but friendly exchange was disastrous to my day.

I would find out much later that the *McKinley* officer on watch had spotted *Sea Sharp II* six miles away and had received orders from the captain to slowly approach my lee side. When I hadn't appeared on deck (thanks to my bare bottom), the captain thought I was sick or hurt or, heaven forbid, no longer aboard.

After the fact, I thought all day about that encounter. Actually, I cried for several hours. I wished I had told the captain about all the breakage, about all my problems. No, I didn't need anything, but certainly I had issues and wants. I could have entertained him with hours of sailor shoptalk.

I wondered about the *McKinley* passengers, about their circumstances back home, about the vacations they were taking to escape those lives on land. I thought of people going to work each morning, to the drudgery of office routines (as I had done for so many years). I wondered what they thought of me in my saggy, baggy, soggy sweat suit when I popped out of the hatch. Before such an abrupt awakening, I had had no one to dress for. Perhaps that's why I spent much of that day sewing while thinking, double-stitching seams on my new dress.

June 5. Talk and talk and talk. How did I talk so much to my recorder and have nothing to say?

I took my third bath of the voyage that day, whoop-de-do! Imagine living with yourself if you had bathed only three times in three weeks. I didn't even wash my hair; I only brushed it. Once a day, I brushed it whether I cared or not.

I saw bunches of gooney birds that day, friendly folks. I swore they knew every time I picked up the can opener. Far and near, those birds came.

The sea that day was full of grayish white vegetation in the shape of chrysanthemums. I wanted to scoop a few into a bucket and bring them on board, but the wake kept them from my reach.

And so the day went. Not much news, but I left a record of each interesting moment on my recorder.

June 6. At 4:00 in the morning, it felt as though *Sea Sharp II* had come to a halt. The sails luffed. I put us back on course, then returned to bed. Five minutes later it happened again. It turned out that the wind vane was slipping in the socket rather than turning the rudder.

After fixing the problem, we sailed at five knots all day. I didn't want to push her any faster. She was most comfortable at that speed, and so was I. It was a drizzly day of brown—yes, brown—air, with steady winds at twenty-eight miles per hour and another falling barometer. I knew what was coming.

By night the wind had grown to a howl, and I stayed dressed when I slipped into bed. No use changing when I knew I'd be out there for who knows how long, fixing who knows what in the coming storm. To me, fear is the unknown. How high will the wind and waves be this time? How long will it last? Will anything else break?

It arrived with winds switching from south-southwest to west-northwest, and up to forty miles per hour. I went out to jibe the mizzen, and it took me forty-five minutes to get the running backstay around the end of the mizzen boom. I tried to grab the running backstay with a boat hook to pull it around, but when the boat lurched on a wave, I dropped the boat hook in the sea. I stood on top of the stern pulpit, clung to the boom crutch, and leaned over the stern, trying to swing it around—one of the stupidest things I'd ever done on a boat. I swore like a proverbial sailor that night.

Within a few hours, we'd spiraled into a full-fledged gale, the third so far. Why, oh why? Hadn't we seen and suffered enough? The winds surpassed fifty miles per hour, and *Sea Sharp II* wasn't behaving her ladylike self. I felt like a cork in boiling water, except that night I shivered. The noise, like high-pitched screams through the rigging, split my eardrums. Silverware clattered back and forth in its drawer. Tools in the toolbox rattled, and cans banged together in storage.

That storm had a mind of its own, I began to believe. It was out to get me; I felt that. I believed that. It was testing my patience, my soul. How much could I take? Like the devil, that storm wanted to know.

I felt a frenzy building. They weren't confused seas. They were malicious. They were pure, calculated turbulence. They were evil, if a storm could be personified and judged. The entire night was a battle of boat against sea, of sails against waves and wind. With every surge, Sea Sharp II was knocked about and the deck deluged with green water.

At 4:00 a.m. I scolded myself. I meant it! We had ourselves a whole gale; I recorded a gust of sixty-eight miles per hour, the worst yet. Water pooled everywhere; the cockpit well filled like a cistern. I confided all to my friendly tape recorder, "Will we see another sunrise?" I swore I was not going outside one more time. Not one more time! I had already reefed the storm trysail and trailed a line astern to slow us a bit, if possible. I wondered if God might be reaching out his hand for me!

Then.

I heard something knocking against the outside of the hull. So out I went again on hands and knees, trying to stop the noise. It was only a small shackle from my little house flag halyard. I returned below with a dry mouth full of cotton. I couldn't stand for Sea Sharp II to be lashed like that, like a beaten girl. It would tackle her ego and mine. She was my friend, my comrade, and I couldn't stand to have her feelings hurt.

While out there, a torrent of water crashed over the deck. The storm continued to grow while I shrank, in dignity anyway. I lost my voice. I couldn't even speak anymore to my recorder. I could only pray: "Please, Lord, I'm sorry to be such a coward. We don't want to die like this, to be washed at sea, swallowed by the storm. Please hold us together and bring this boat home. . . ."

June 7. The sea crashed a dreadful crash that morning. It wasn't the wind; it was water. I thought the bottom had ripped from the boat. It took several seconds before *Sea Sharp II* righted herself, but it felt like forever. I thought it was the end. I thought we were finished. A wave had knocked us over and laid us flat, ninety degrees. I'm sure the port spreader hit the water. It was my fault for getting caught parallel in a trough.

Then I realized: I was still breathing; I remained in one piece.

The padding had saved me, but the cabin was a shambles. Everything was shaken and stirred, like a martini with delicate ice. Books lay atop me; and ironically, the radio was on, playing Tiny Tim's version of "Tiptoe through the Tulips."

Wash your face and smile.

That was my mantra, the maxim I'd been told all my childhood. And that's precisely what I did. I wiped my face with a cold cloth, and I tried to smile amid the blows. There was power in a smile. I would pretend the ordeal had never happened.

But I could not ignore such destruction in my pretty boat; in fact, I'd be looking for things for a long while. I found the strangest items in the oddest places. My broom, normally by the entry, was forward by the head. I found food everywhere, no longer in cupboard order: vegetables with fruit, meat with juice, and soup with nuts.

My nerves were close to breaking; I really had to get some sleep. Also, I had torn a hole in the lower batten pocket of the mizzen sail, so it needed a patch. Later. Problem was, there was always something to think about, and I just couldn't keep up with all those things. And when all the thinking was done, there was always room left over for worry.

But right then, I needed sleep.

June 8. I managed to get nearly nine hours in bed, waking only twice to check the cabin compass. And then, sunlight dazzled the deck. We had made it through another night, I was rested, and it was time to fix all that had broken.

First things first, I raised the sails. Then, I whipped open every drawer, every cupboard, and every locker to dry out. I emptied all the contents and spread half of them across the deck in the fresh air and sunlight, same routine once again. I took the mizzen sail off the boom to patch the batten pocket. I had a new sail-mending kit with me, a gift from a lovable eighty-year-old man named Mizuno, who had made my mainsail, mizzen, and trysail. I could picture him in my memory, dressed in flowing black, gnarled old hands molded from years of sewing canvas on sailing ships. Somehow my sewing seemed so trivial compared with his.

The more I tidied, the more I found things out of place. How could a deck brush with a five-foot handle fly from the port to the starboard lazarette? It would take me at least a day to straighten out the toolbox, like a tackle box with forty-eight compartments and four tiers. Nuts, bolts, washers, pliers, wrenches, screw drivers, hammers, hacksaw, hand drill, files, you name it, they were all messed up; little nuts on the bottom, big tools on top, everything was all a jumble.

I worked on the wind vane, tightening a bolt to stop a squeak. And I had to hunt for my Timex watch and navigation dividers, which I finally found lurking behind the toilet.

It figured I'd whack my head again. Just as the lump on my forehead disappeared, I acquired another behind my ear. I thought I would put the mainsail back up in case a breeze came through in the night. I momentarily raised my head when I shouldn't have, and the sheet block caught me. Good thing it wasn't the boom, or I'd have been out of the game. Before sailing, I never knew I could be such a danger to myself.

But there was good news that night: I took a longitude reading from the sunset and learned the international date line lay thirty miles away, perhaps within a day's reach. I'm sure that newfound knowledge of our position factored into my outlook, but I swear that sunset on June 8 was the most beautiful I'd ever seen—brilliant red and orange reflecting off every wrinkle in the sea, as though we were crossing a wavy field of flowers.

The next day would mark four weeks since our departure from Japan. Five years before that, I had never dreamt of seeing Japan. Five years before I started sailing, I had never imagined I would see the South Pacific. It all seemed so unreal to me. I had seen and done so much through sailing. I had lived a life I never before imagined, yet I forged ahead in isolation, without any proof to the rest of the world that I still existed.

June 9. Such a calm night. We traveled only four miles, and at times almost backward. But I slept again, in quiet peace. I awoke to another stunning sky of glistening silver with a hint of yellow, growing brighter then morphing into various shades of pink. The colors seemed to come from a fountain, spewing into the sky, announcing the commencement of another day.

By 11:30 the sun beamed overhead, not a cloud about. It was an easy, uneventful ride across the date line. I would never have known had I not understood the chart. There should have been a bump! Or a flag in the sea! It was such a milestone, yet the water flowed on as ever, in every direction. No matter, the crossing was such a feat to me that I felt as though a great burden had been lifted from my mind; I got goose bumps and tingles. And the next morning, I would wake to June 9 for the second time.

A little celebration was in order. I ate the last two brandy balls from my Wednesday Box. As if on cue, a group of porpoises swooped gracefully about the boat, nuzzling each other and rolling through the sea. Their slippery backs glistened in the sun like polished chrome. They seemed to smile at me and talk in their squeaky voices, saying, "Welcome to this side of the world."

What a day. I wouldn't have swapped it with anyone, for anything. The news was full of President Nixon, who happened to have been in Midway, where he met the Republic of Vietnam president Nguyen Van Thieu and announced the policy of "Vietnamization," building up South Vietnamese forces to take over the war. But Nixon would have to continue his trip without us. I wasn't going to pay him a visit. I had decided to keep going, heading home toward California.

That decided, I consulted Horie's book again. He had one typhoon and four gales before the date line; I'd had six gales. But Horie had nothing after the date line. In his book, he described how the seas seemed to build before the wind rose, how the wind circled continuously rather than blowing from one direction. That's the way it was. He survived. I determined it would be no worse for me.

June 9 (all over again). I'd make the day shorter. I'd make it twenty-two hours long and gain some daylight savings time. I could do that at sea; I could change my clock as I wanted, so long as I kept meticulous track of the hours in my logbook. I could make the sun set at 8:30 rather than 6:30; I could make it rise at 5:30 rather than 3:30. It didn't matter. Time was nebulous, except for navigation. After all, longitude really is time.

The previous night passed calmly and beautifully, in darkness with no moon. I loved those nights, when looking down into the water appeared the same as looking up to the heavens, the entire world awhirl with trillions of stars and their reflections.

I spent that duplicate June 9 doing womanly things I rarely had time for—a manicure, a pedicure, attention to my cuticles and calluses, a shaving of the legs, a plucking of the eyebrows, a little trimming of the hair.

June 10.
And June 11.
And June 12.
And June 13.

On and on it went, a dismal stretch that began on the tenth at 4:00 a.m. (of course!) despite my daylight savings attempt. Light fog and misty rain made it a gray and clammy day, which would stretch for ten more. Nothing in the sky changed but the density of fog or intensity of drizzle for a week and a half. Plus, the sea rolled and swelled the entire time. I hated those hours (which would turn to days), all blurring together in an oppressive gloom. I felt claustrophobic, depressed. I hated my clothes. It was fifty-eight degrees and damp; I didn't know if warmth would be possible again. Even my sleeping bag felt clammy when I first climbed into it. When I finally felt snug and dry, I never wanted to leave.

I found three squid washed up on the deck. I never knew a squid had such a pretty face. They seemed to have come with the rain. I rather liked them, so I put them in a bucket of water to see if they would last until I could take a picture when it stopped raining.

Several times that day, I heard about Heyerdahl attempting his crossing from Morocco to Barbados in a papyrus boat. It was all over the radio news. Heyerdahl had a crew of seven! Why wasn't anyone concerned about me, alone? It had been more than a week since the *McKinley* spotted me, yet I'd heard nothing. Nothing on the radio. Was it because I was a woman?

It was a lousy day, and I would just chalk it up to that. Better to give in and admit it than to fight it; it wasn't going to change. So I told my trusty recorder all about it. Then I went on an inspection tour, and in the forward cabin, I found my suitcase so moldy it seemed to have sprouted across the bunk. I should have shipped it home by plane, high and dry in the sky. That was foolish of me. So, there I had ruined an $80 suitcase and half my clothes.

Mold, mildew, little growing things everywhere. The anchor line had sprouted three-inch whiskers; I couldn't do anything about the problem until the sun returned.

I didn't know what to do, bellow or cry or run outside and

keep on running. I wasn't being melodramatic; I just didn't know how I'd keep going. If only I could open the hatch, get warm for a while, stop the boat from rolling, for just a few minutes. If only I could keep to our course. I swear I put on and took off, put on and took off, put on and took off my foul-weather gear five hundred times that day. I changed the wind vane or trimmed sails every twenty minutes for fourteen hours.

That day, I spotted a glass fishing float in the water. I watched it bob around us. It was crusted like a floating mine, but I wanted it. I jibed the boat to go pick it up. It meant resetting every single line and retrimming the sails and wind vane. It took more than an hour, but it was worth it. It was the highlight of my day. I just keep telling myself to take one day at a time, but some days required immense stamina. I had to find interest or comfort or pleasure in small things, in the insignificant, like a derelict fishnet float. I would keep that little float for years to come, a conversation piece in my living room.

I heated my dinner twice that night. I had just warmed leftover ham with peas and carrots when I was driven outside again by a change in the wind. By the time I returned, the food was cold. I re-heated the dinner—and I don't even like peas and carrots—and sat with the warm pan in my lap. It was the best warmth I had that day.

According to my dead reckoning, we'd passed the halfway mark to San Diego, but I felt no need to rejoice. I was cold. I could see my breath in the cabin. I told my tape recorder about spilling coffee on the carpet when the boat had a sudden lurch. I knew it would never be clean again. I said Clair would have to replace it, if I ever got that boat to California. I couldn't sharpen my pencils, they were so damp. Have you ever tried writing on soggy paper?

None of that helped my disposition. And I had to add two more things to my list of things gone wrong. When I was on deck at 2:30 a.m., I discovered the spreader lights didn't work. I went forward to remove the whisker pole from the staysail in total darkness. I couldn't see my hands in front of my face. A black shroud had been draped around the boat, and I was suffocating beneath it. I took apart the spreader light, found it one big corroded mess, cleaned it out, sprayed it with WD-40, and put it back together. It still didn't work. The fuses were OK; had I broken a wire? I wished I had studied electronics.

Then came the most disturbing news of all—reading my log, I discovered I hadn't bathed in nine days. I normally washed my hair every five days, but I couldn't remember the last time I had. It was so cold; there was no way would I douse myself in seawater. So I checked the calendar, and guess what! Nine days. I heated a teakettle of rainwater; and while it warmed, I washed my hair in the toilet. That way I didn't have to go outside. Why not? I just pumped seawater into the head, and rinsed with the warm. Think what you will—I felt so much better.

I knew we'd traveled halfway in distance, but I had no idea whether we'd reached the halfway point in time. I flipped my pillowcase inside out, hoping it would be a little cleaner. I had packed only two, and I didn't know how long each would have to last. It's amazing what a sailor gives up at sea, what people take for granted on land.

For hours, for days, it rained. The sky was gray. The boat pitched. I did almost nothing. No shopping, no movies, no luncheons with friends. No parties, no bottles of wine. I had a bad hankering for a sandwich with fresh bread, mayo, crisp lettuce, and a thick, thick slab of cheese. (Those visions would taunt me.) I vowed to ask for cheese if another ship came by.

But what else could I do?

I thought about my friends.

I wondered how they were.

I wondered whether they thought of me.

I wondered what gossip I'd missed.

I wondered how much time I could kill by thinking.

But I had to watch my thoughts. I knew if I thought too long about loved ones on land, I'd slide into a depression. So I made plans instead. I thought about returning home. I would put on weight (what a goal!). I'd go out every night, and I wouldn't sit home for one minute alone. I'd talk to friends, and maybe they'd actually talk back—not like the gooney birds that entertained me in silence. Those birds were cute, but they had nothing much to say in my language. Nor like the wind vane, which I spoke to frequently, telling it how magnificent it was and how good it had been to me. Not much of a conversationalist there, either.

Sometimes I actually enjoyed the fog. It was so thick some nights that I didn't turn on an outside light. I couldn't have been seen anyway, so I conserved energy. When the rain stopped, the air went silent, like a stalker.

Sometimes I waged war against things that didn't matter. Have you ever been infuriated by a screw top that won't come off a jar? In the middle of the ocean, it's unbearable. You wrench your hands around that jar, strain every muscle, and yank and pull and curse the damn thing, scraping the skin off your knuckles. Still, there's absolutely nothing you can do. And there's absolutely no one around to hear your screams or to rush to your aid.

I should have been happier at that point. I shouldn't have been cursing little jars, because I changed charts. I'd passed from the one with only ocean on it, to another with land at the far right. California was on the map at last! At least I knew I couldn't miss an entire continent. I'd hit land eventually; it was right there, on the fringes of my chart.

June 21. Lots to do that day since the sun returned, as did a blue sky. I awoke to a light breeze, easy seas, and a change in the atmosphere. A tiny strip of pink stretched across the horizon, to my utmost amazement. It was sixty-one degrees.

But good moods never lasted. Later that day, I feared the engine had chugged its last. I tried to start it so I could charge the batteries for my running lights—but nothing happened. I did the whole routine: opened the exhaust valve, turned the master switch on, and rolled the key over one notch for twenty seconds. I inspected below, and all looked good as far as I could tell, except for a slight drip from the water intake assembly. Nothing seemed to solve the puzzle. I really knew nothing about diesel engines. I didn't need the engine, but as long as Clair had had it installed, I figured I might as well take advantage of the luxury for running lights. I had kerosene lamps, of course, which the boatyard metal smith had made for me. But I really didn't like them—messy, stinky things.

June 23. What a difference a day makes. I awoke to a sea exactly as I had left it—deep blue with little white caps studding the water like diamonds. It took six weeks, but I'd finally found the sailing I had dreamed of. We traveled at more than four knots, but it felt like *Sea Sharp II* just sat in the water, perfectly in sync with the wind. Such seas didn't come around very often. How frustrating, though, not having anyone with whom I could share the moment.

I worked on navigation that day and figured we'd averaged 538 miles per week at 3.2 knots for a total of 3,230 miles. That would put us home on July 20. I must have been heading home. I heard it on the radio, very faintly, broadcasts from Salt Lake City and Maui—straight and clear from the USA!

But I still hadn't heard a report on *Sea Sharp II*, nor any question of our whereabouts.

June 24. It was the whitest night I'd ever seen. The moon was obscured by a sheath of fog, but the sky and water were one, all white, which was much better than dark and dismal.

What an odd fog we had that day, with visibility down to a few hundred yards but a crown of blue sky overhead as though we moved encased in a tube. It was damp, too, with condensation dripping from the sails. The thermometer read seventy-eight degrees, and I was warm enough to wear almost nothing on deck. Finally, I felt fine air on my naked skin. What an overdue pleasure!

And I had neighbors! I didn't see them, but a beer can floated by. Someone else was out there in my ocean.

June 25. I should have known the wind would die as soon as I made predictions of our arrival. We logged twenty-four miles that day, and everything grew worse after that.

June 26. I made a new friend. As I swept the carpet that morning, I heard a "plop" beside the boat. There, just a few inches from the hull, was a gooney bird paddling beside us. He was all alone, no friends in sight. I dug up a package of crackers for him; and as soon as he gulped down a piece, more gooneys came from every direction, zooming in around the boat for breakfast. *Sea Sharp II* was only a little faster than they were; and as soon as we got away from the birds, I'd drop another cracker overboard, and they'd run, run, run across the water in a frenzy! My stomach ached from laughing so hard.

This continued through the noon hour, at which point seventeen birds had joined the party. They ate all the crackers I had. I sprinkled crumbs into the water, and they went after those, too. I sat with my recorder in the cockpit, taping their voices. Gooneys are amazing birds. They undergo highly stylized, elaborate mating dances in an effort to find a partner for life. Each gooney couple then creates a unique language for themselves.

I noticed one of the birds had a band around his leg. I named him George, and he became my friend. By dinnertime the birds still paddled beside us, George in the lead. He would paddle to the bow of the boat, look back, and let out a loud *squaaaaawk*. "Can't you even keep up?" he seemed to say. The fact that they were still there, keeping astride, told me just how slow we were going.

I spent most of the day with those birds, recording them and filming them—only to discover hours later that my camera had no film.

June 27. First thing I did, I went straight on deck. Sure enough, George and eight friends continued to float along. I'd grown rather fond of them. When I took my breakfast into the cockpit to watch them, I realized we had another visitor: a four-foot gray shark. The gooneys didn't even pay attention. The shark was graceful, swooping around the keel with seamless effort.

The ocean looked like a mirror that day. It's incredible to imagine the constant changing of the sea, which has such smoothness one day, such torment the next. It was so calm that day; the water perfectly reflected the gooneys on the surface. The only sound was the slatting sails.

Later that afternoon, I spotted the most unusual shark, which had a red stripe down its back. I'd never seen one like that. I asked George if he knew what it was—and then I realized the shark had acquired its red stripe from the bottom paint on *Sea Sharp II* while going after the barnacles collected there. That shark wasn't so friendly, circling slowly, then jerking around. It left briefly, then returned with four friends. "Look what I found!" he must have told them.

June 28. Another day of battle. I spent the morning with circling winds—trimming sails, and trimming sails again as the wind came from every direction, then left us completely.

By the afternoon, I'd cleaned everything aboard, fixed everything broken, greased everything that needed greasing. I'd polished the chrome and prettied myself. Even George had grown tired of our slow progress. There was nothing more I could do.

So I waited.

For something.

For air.

My mind kept asking "Will the wind ever blow again? Am I to be a floating derelict forever? Just more flotsam on the open sea?"

June 29. I didn't want to say good morning that day. Since the evening before, the log told me we'd traveled three-quarters of a mile—in circles. The sails, hanging limp and useless, kept me awake most the night. I never should have predicted a date for San Diego.

That night, I listened to radio from Portland, San Francisco, Albuquerque, and Los Angeles. Great, they still existed. But did I?

June 30. I sat on the bow that morning, watching a shark at the edge of the boat eyeing us fervently. We were covered in barnacles and moss on the port side, which had had more shade than the starboard side. We'd sprouted a colony down there, so I set to work hanging over the edge and scraping it off with a paring knife. I had tried the deck brush, but the handle broke. The knife worked, but I couldn't reach very far. I wasn't about to jump in, knowing sharks still lurked about. So paring knife it was.

July 1. Life had changed again. We moved! We logged twelve miles in the five hours I'd slept the night before. I tore June off the calendar and celebrated in our progress.

But the sky darkened in midaftternoon as a squall approached from the north. I took the main down, though we had only had a few drops of rain. After all my mishaps, I was still overly cautious and a bit of a coward.

By nightfall I glimpsed a freighter heading west, lit up like a birthday cake. It could have been two miles away, though it was hard to say exactly. I shined my beam straight toward it, pointed my light at my own sails and swung it around a few times, hoping I'd grab someone's attention. I wasn't signaling, just hoping to be seen.

Apparently, my efforts failed.

July 2. July 3. Same old same old. These were nothing but two straight days of aggravation, not enough wind for me to tack, which left me constantly trimming sails. I cried. I went to bed and told *Sea Sharp II* to do whatever she darned well pleased.

July 4. I didn't even have a firecracker to celebrate Independence Day. It was a nice day, with winds finally blowing from the northeast, but there would be no picnic for me that holiday.

I'd started running out of batteries; I thought I'd brought twice as many as I would need. The tape recorder took five; the spotlight, six; the radio, nine; and the flashlights, two each. Should it have come to it, I would have foregone light before abandoning my recorder or radio; they were my only connections to the world.

News flash: I saw another sailboat way off on the horizon. We were about 1,800 miles from San Francisco with nothing around, when I popped my head out and there she was, maybe twice the length of *Sea Sharp II*. We were both on the same tack, but who knows where my new friend was headed. I wondered about that boat and the people aboard. Who were they? Did they wonder the same of me? Did they even see me? I was so excited about a boat even as far away as that one was, and chances were, they didn't even see me. "Grand Central Station out here," I spoke to my tape recorder. "What's to become of the traffic?"

That night, we suffered another problem—no running lights at all. The kerosene lights wouldn't work because one glass hurricane lamp had broken. I dug out my spares only to find them useless. In Japan I had drawn a pattern of the twelve replacements I wanted, but something didn't translate. They must have thought, well, if she wants four inches, eight inches would be twice as good.

No dice. They were too big. So we sailed dark, which didn't matter in the vacuous middle of the sea. But I would have to figure out something before reaching the coast. I would think about that another day.

July 5–9. There was not much to report. No good news, no bad news. It took the entirety of those five days for the wind to switch to the south, to push us in the direction we wanted to go. In two weeks, we'd covered 364 miles, well under par.

July 10. And the world turned. Ours did, anyway. We'd traveled 111 miles since the previous day. We were shooting through the water at seven knots; we were going so fast I had to slow her down. I lowered the mizzen and furled the staysail to half its size, which still kept us at five knots.

That morning, I had awoken at 5:30 and jumped on deck in my birthday suit, which would have been no big deal. But right there on the starboard side was a massive tanker heading west, tossing an enormous wave. I'd never seen such a big ship so close, speeding along so fast. Two minutes later we were pitched in its wake. What a bruise to this little boat's ego. I told my recorder, "I hope they have two navigators on board—one for the bow and one for the stern."

July 11. For the past sixty days, I'd been using a Citizen watch that counted backward. At the start of my trip, I set it for eighty, and it counted down the days. But I couldn't bear to see such high numbers, so I covered the face. On July 10, I knew it would say twenty days, a bearable number—though longer than I thought it would take—so I removed the tape. No end to the tricks the mind will play.

July 12. At noon my logbook read, "4,758 miles. Compass course: 90 degrees. Barometer: 30.9. Temperature: 74 degrees. Weather: high, overcast. Wind: northwest, 10 mph. Remarks: Changed course for home. Point Arguello, here we come!"

I had been two months at sea.

I started doing math in my head—all sorts of wild calculations. I had 1,029 miles to go. If we sailed eighty miles per day, we'd be home on the morning of July 25, which would mean another twelve and three-quarters days, or 309 more hours. Could I really figure such things? Of course not. But I tried.

I listened to San Francisco's KNBR all morning. I heard about Donald Crowhurst, an Englishman who was sailing around the world in the *Sunday Times* Golden Globe Race. He had gone ashore in South America and started reporting false positions. The other racers continued on around the world. On their way back, Crowhurst joined them back at sea for the rest of the journey home. His boat, the *Teignmouth Electron*, was found with sails set, dinghy and life raft aboard, but no Donald. Insanity presumably took him. He left behind detailed logbooks and startling confessions of his lies.

What drove such sailors to the edge? What really happened in the end? So many seafarers have vanished in mystery. William Willis was another. He had navigated several *Kon-Tiki*-like expeditions, living for months at a time on a balsa-wood raft, subsisting on olive oil and flour. He had been around the world several times during his seafaring life. And then while trying to cross the Atlantic, his boat was found sailing along without him. You ask yourself: Was it accident? Did the boom knock him over? Was this his final wish to become one with his beloved sea? Had he hit one of those nasty lows when the wind doesn't blow or the sun doesn't shine or the solitude eats at the mind? The doldrums could get a sailor. Self-destruction was less likely in a storm because something was always happening; there was always something to fight. But from the drudgery of a windless week or an eternity of gray days, you could go right out of your mind.

I listened to the radio more and grew a little jealous. Every hour, there was something on Thor Heyerdahl. And I heard about Eric Tabarly, a notable French single-hander. Great achievers, to be sure, but what about that woman out there? Sour grapes. I felt sorry for myself again, and that simply wouldn't do.

So I started thinking, "Would there be another voyage like this for me?"

July 13. I heard my name. That afternoon, the announcer on the 12:30 news said I hadn't been seen in forty days, not since the *McKinley* had talked to me. I hadn't been forgotten after all! They reported me. They remembered me. That meant I existed.

July 14. I was so —— mad that it was a good thing no one could hear me screaming. I hadn't had a good navigational reading in four days, and I needed one. We were making such good time, ever closer to shore. Just as I was trying to take a sextant shot, the wind switched, the boat rolled, and I flew against the hatch—I was getting lax and careless. Then a cloud obscured the sun, and I didn't get my reading after all.

I was growing more and more worried about approaching shore. What if no one came to greet us? I had no lights. I'd have to stay awake and sail through the dark in heavy shipping lanes. Several sailors had said they would come out and go down the coast with me to be my eyes when I was off shore. I was counting on their word.

July 15. I'd grown so antsy, I took a mild tranquilizer. In twenty hours, we'd sailed a hundred miles. I didn't want to go so fast. At that rate, we'd hit land before midnight on the eighteenth, and I wanted to arrive in daylight.

The wind revved to thirty miles per hour, well within the realm of small-craft warning weather! By midnight we were 250 miles off San Francisco as the crow flies; that was as close as we'd get to the KGO radio station, which came in loud and clear. I could hear the Long Beach Coast Guard, the San Pedro marine operator, and the San Francisco operator on my Zenith shortwave receiver—it was consolation to me. But since I couldn't talk to them, what good did that consolation do me?

July 16. I was up at 5:00 a.m. listening to *Apollo 11* blast off for the moon. I could just picture America in front of the TV, millions of people with their eyes glued to that historic sight. I was suddenly reminded of TVs, cars, freeways, phones, running water. I'd have quite a transition to normal life again.

July 17. No sign of anyone or anything for several days, except a piece of lumber covered in barnacles. What happened to all the fishing boats? Where did they go? Why was I still alone?

I was getting close enough to land that I felt I could probably scream and people would hear me. In forty-eight hours I'd see the coast. Then the most incredible thoughts came. Do I really want to end this journey? Am I ready to go home now? Maybe I'd just stay out here a while longer until I could ease into land life again. I rushed below to tell my friendly tape recorder but then thought otherwise: "No, I didn't really mean it. I didn't mean it." Really, I wanted to go home.

Back to reality. I'd talked my way through storms and doldrums, so maybe I could talk my way through to San Diego. I couldn't predict the low visibility we would have later, but at that moment the air was perfectly clear around us. Yet a light brown smudge traced the horizon behind us; we had sailed through a curtain of smog. We had to be close to California.

I had thought that when a big ship spotted a small sailboat in the middle of the ocean, it would report the sighting. Apparently not. Maybe they hadn't spotted me. According to the news, I'd still not been seen since the *McKinley*, so no one knew I was so close to California at that very moment. And land presented trouble for me. H-E-L-L. I spelled it out. It was 2:00 a.m. and I hadn't slept, keeping my eyes open for passing ships.

Then the wind dropped to nothing. We didn't move. We certainly wouldn't reach the coast in the dark, putting most of my worries to rest. For a while.

July 18. We drifted all night, circling twice, sitting in a little puff of air from the north. Then nothing. The wind couldn't make up its mind, and the sun hadn't even tried to burn the fog away. How lazy was that? Yet it was daytime, and that's when I wanted to move. We drifted for hours, and at 4:00 p.m. I had excitement: a honeybee aboard the boat. That's how close to land we were.

By evening I had no words, no respectable way to describe the day, so I described what I did: I kicked, I beat my fists, I slammed my pans, and I raised a ruckus that did no iota of good. I could have taken a hammer to the boat and beaten it to death. I screamed all the naughty words I knew, until I was hoarse. That's how mad I was. I was so close, so very close to home, yet we weren't going anywhere.

July 19. I had a good talk with myself and explained to *Sea Sharp II* that that was how it was meant to be. There had to be a reason for the seemingly senseless drifting, just beyond the cusp of being offshore.

I saw porpoises that day. I saw several big sharks, floating kelp, a cabbage head, and onions. Litter from land provided signs of other life.

I used an entire gallon of water to bathe and wash my hair. I put on clean jeans and a sweatshirt, hoping I'd feel better. I'd planned on waiting until we were truly offshore before I prettied my face and nails, but I couldn't stand myself any longer.

At 3:00 p.m. I spotted a fisherman way off our bow, zigzagging back and forth. I waved a red towel at him and gave a few long blasts of my horn. I did everything but stand on my head and do cartwheels. But no. At 7:00 p.m. he was still out there, ignoring me. I guessed we were about forty-five miles from Point Arguello. No lights. No wind. No response.

FOURTEEN

A Pink Return

July 20. Sunday morning began with the sound of a whale breathing. Have you ever heard one? It's an extraordinary gush. Whales only breathe once or twice a minute, and they release almost all of their oxygen when they exhale. They push out that air with such force, it forms a spout and turns to vapor when their moist breath reaches the outside air. I whispered into my recording, hoping I wouldn't disturb it. It was so foggy I couldn't tell water from sky. I couldn't see much, but I could make out the sleek form of that whale as it rose to the surface. It was sharing the waters with birds, porpoises, and a single seal. We were definitely near land.

9:43 a.m. I would never believe that last ship hadn't seen me standing out there on deck trying to get its attention. It came straight toward us then veered to avoid a collision. I seethed with anger. All I wanted was someone to radio the news that I had arrived.

10:24 a.m. I had the strongest smell of land, a good old fishy sea-weed smell. And off the bow, I heard a foghorn. I kept listening.

11:00 a.m. I didn't care what anyone said, it was a diaphone, a fog-horn. I'd been out on the bowsprit listening for more than thirty minutes, and I was certain. It couldn't be a ship's signal because its intervals were less than two minutes. So whose diaphone was it? Point Arguello lighthouse was what I had been aiming for all along, for my first sighting of land. It was dead ahead according to my calculations. It was! It had to be!

12:50 a.m. I still heard the diaphone, which was growing louder. I heard other noises, too, including a roaring sound. We were heading directly for the diaphone, and I stared in that direction, though all I saw was fog. Only eight hours of daylight remained, and in that time I would arrive in the shipping lanes, the passage of water between the mainland and the chain of offshore islands. It was so eerie. I expected to see breakers anytime, suddenly ap-pearing ahead of us. That would mean disaster.

1:45 p.m. Land! Yes, that was land ahead.

3:00 p.m. It was Arguello, for sure, and July 20 was my lucky day. Another fishing boat was heading north up the coast, so I was on the bowsprit again trying to rally its attention. I almost fell over-board when the boat changed course and motored toward us.

It must have been obvious I wasn't a leisurely Sunday sailor, Sunday though it was. We were still a foreign vessel entering U.S. waters, so I had dressed our boat for the occasion. I raised the quarantine flag on the starboard side, with my house flag below. Of course, my precious American flag was flying as it had for seventy days; and for fun, I raised two three-foot Japanese carp windsocks to the masthead. It is the Japanese custom to fly one for each boy and girl in the family on May 5, Children's Day. They are meant to bring health and prosperity. I flew one for Sandy and one for Dennis.

"Did you want something?" the skipper asked, as he came alongside.

"I've just sailed from Japan," my voice quivered. It had been forty-eight days since my last conversation—"Yes. No. Thank you," to the *McKinley* captain. I had hoped to carry this conversation with ease, an effortless exchange between two captains at sea. But when I opened my mouth, it was a voice that sounded strange to my own ears. I breathed deeply before continuing.

"Would you mind sending a message for me?"

It was the *Little Swede*, heading to Oregon waters for salmon. The captain was Bob Spicker; his mate, Pat Cannon. Those guys were good to me. They stayed with me for forty-five minutes, trying without success to reach Los Angeles by radiotelephone. Finally, they talked to a fisherman friend, up the coast in Morro Bay, who promised to go ashore and make my call.

"You sure have a lot of friends with you," Pat nodded toward the water beside me.

I looked to the side and saw two porpoises playing at the bow and a big seal flapping at the transom. We watched the circus for a while, mesmerized, until Bob and Pat said they really must go. They wished me well, waved good-bye, and set off only to turn around again.

"We forgot to ask if there's anything you need."

What I needed most—to be found—had already been taken care of.

But July 20, of course, went down in history not as the historic day when I, Sharon Sites Adams, first spotted land but as the day that man walked on the moon. Sitting under the stars in the cockpit, I listened to Walter Cronkite and his coverage. To think! I made landfall just as Neil Armstrong took that giant step. A few furry clouds drifted overhead, but I could see that moon clearly.

On through the hours while watching that moon, I thought of the times I was growing up when that big old fellow brightened a night sky; I always wondered if those pioneers in their covered wagons on the way to Oregon had enjoyed the moonlight as much as I did. I always wished that I could have been one of them. I was born seventy-five years too late—or fifty years too early. Even before that day, I had given thought to how exciting it would be as an astronaut, breaking new territory. Do you suppose Neil Armstrong would have changed places with me right then?

I wished, then, that my sailing had made some contribution to science or that I'd discovered something remarkable or invented something useful for humanity. But it didn't, and I hadn't. I hadn't done anything but bring an idea to fruition. The journey fulfilled my own wishes, and maybe I'd be setting a world record. But I wasn't charting new worlds.

Or was I?

As I made my approach that night, I had no recourse but to run dark. I would hang a white flashlight in the rigging. It was all I had. Not legal, of course, but maybe someone would see it, keeping me from being run down. Better than nothing, I figured.

Midnight. I couldn't keep awake—my heavy eyes kept wanting to shut. The current was taking us inshore. I could see lights, dazzling lights in the distance. I could see headlights going up and down the highway on land. I heard an ambulance speeding toward Santa Barbara. I could see the Point Conception light and two oil rigs illuminated like Christmas trees. Farther out in the shipping lanes, there were six vessels. I had my spotlight ready to shine on my sails, just in case someone came closer. And I finally solved the mystery noise, which hadn't been my imagination but the rumbling of a train on land, as I discovered when another one went by.

There I was, so close to humanity that I could hear its comings and goings. I was beginning to wonder whether my message had made it. I still hadn't heard anything on the news. Nothing about me.

July 21. 4:00 a.m. We tacked four times as the light breeze came from the precise direction in which we wanted to go. I took three pills to stay awake. My eyelids felt as though they were lifting weights. If I hadn't heard by daylight that someone had received my message, I'd have to flag down another fisherman.

9:30 a.m. I hove to and set the alarm for an hour later. I was so tired, but I couldn't sleep.

10:05 a.m. They knew! I heard it on KNX and ABC. No blaring trumpets, no fanfare, just the news: "Sharon Adams in her thirty-one-foot sailboat has been sighted off the California coast."
At last!

Noon. Still no wind, but there was plenty of hot sun, even through lifting fog. I was getting my first suntan of the year. I felt like a baked potato on drugs. A small plane circled above, and a cameraman took pictures. I waved briefly, but my mind was on other things. I had other problems to contend with.

When the plane first appeared, I was on the foredeck getting the anchor ready. *Sea Sharp II* was close-hauled and trying to make headway, but there was not even a fickle breath of air. We drifted all morning toward shore. I spotted a kelp bed and a pair of white breakers, much too close. I would have hated to end up on the beach after six thousand miles.

1:00 p.m. We finally got a little breeze and went along our merry way. *Sea Sharp II* did her job, holding perfect course for another three hours. I napped for forty-five minutes, then awoke abruptly, sensing danger. We had just slipped past an oil rig on the starboard side. Not ten feet from our stern was a black mooring can used by the tenders. The men on board looked startled to see us, but their expressions didn't compare with mine when I realized *Sea Sharp II*, all on her own, had steered us safely through the maze. Another angel at the helm.

6:00 p.m. As I was fixing a quick dinner below deck, I changed the radio station to ABC for some reason.

"After this commercial we'll have a word with Al Adams. He is aboard the *Aikane*, heading up the coast."

Marv Gray, the announcer, returned a minute later. "Al, you tell me this is Sharon's favorite station, so I'm going to give you the chance to talk to her. Go ahead. Let's hope she's listening."

He told me to turn my spreader lights on and blink them intermittently through the night. I should keep a sharp lookout because he and my friends would be doing the same.

What could I do? I was being told what to do, but I couldn't talk back. I didn't have spreader lights. I didn't have any lights. *Aikane* was farther offshore than we were, the fog was settling in, and we would never find each other.

I had no intention of navigating through that traffic to head farther offshore, looking for *Aikane*. I couldn't do anything but turn eastward, follow the coastline south, and try to hail another boat off Santa Barbara. The sun was setting before I got that far. Then a sailboat came our way, and I was anxiously waving a greeting as they came alongside.

"Sharon Sites! Fancy meeting you here!" the woman yelled to me. The last time she'd seen me, she said, I had spoken to her yacht club. It was right after my sail to Hawaii. "We heard you were off the coast, but never expected to see you. What can we do for you?"

Alleluia!

I was growing comfortable with conversation again, so I explained the story. I needed her to call the Santa Barbara harbor-master and ask him to call the San Pedro marine operator, who in turn would be able to send a message to the *Aikane*. "Tell them our present position is off the Santa Barbara breakwater. I have no lights, and I'm sailing inshore down the coast."

How about that—a whole string of words had flowed from my mouth naturally. The woman took the tiller while her husband called. Everything was under control. They wished me luck and continued their trip north to San Francisco.

It was no more than half an hour when another boat came by. "I've been looking for you all day." He was a sailor out of Santa Barbara. "I heard you were coming down from Arguello and just knew if I crisscrossed the channel I'd find you. How are you?"

"Just fine, thank you."

"How was your trip?"

"Just great. A little breakage but nothing I couldn't manage." He wanted a summary of seventy-four days? Impossible.

Here's a little secret: I had a chart for the wide Pacific but had somehow forgotten one for the California coast. I was familiar with the area after having sailed it several times, but still, I should have had a chart. I asked the sailor for a compass course to Port Hueneme. He told me the way and wished me well, and we parted. And then I promptly forgot his name. I forgot the names of the couple who radioed the marine operator for me. I forgot who they were, but I never forgot their kindness.

9:00 p.m. A breeze stuck with us, and we made good time. But visibility diminished. I'd been searching for blinking lights but saw nothing offshore. I grew tired, so tired from the previous day's exhaustion; I just wanted to sleep for a week.

Midnight. Curiosity does wonders. It kept me awake, in suspense. I listened to the ship-to-shore communications and heard the *Aikane* calling in with reports on its search for me.

"It's like looking for a needle in a haystack. Over."

"You'll have to send another boat if you can't make contact with them," another voice radioed. "We're on the shore side of the oil rig between Anacapa Island and Port Hueneme. Over and out."

I could see a flicker in the distance. They wouldn't see me coming since *Sea Sharp II* and I sailed in the dark without lights. It would be fun. We'd sail right up to their side, and I'd call out, "Hey, where have you been? I've been looking all over for you."

But it didn't happen that way. The wind dropped and it was 3:00 a.m. By then, no one was in sight. I decided to head toward Hueneme to see if I could find someone there. I began steering in that direction, but there wasn't enough breeze to push us along. So . . . there . . . we . . . sat. . . .

Again.

July 22. Dawn. "Excuse me for breaking into your conversation, but this is the Port Hueneme harbormaster, and I've been hearing you through the night."

He was speaking to the *Aikane*.

"Are you by any chance looking for a sailboat with a red stripe on the sail? Over."

"Yes, we are! Have you seen it? Over."

"I'm looking at it right now. She's sitting about a mile offshore. Over."

I was drained, mentally and physically. It had been forty-seven hours since I last crawled out of my sleeping bag. I sat in the cockpit, resting my head on my arms with a look of despair. And then I looked up. The bare masts of a sailboat nosed directly toward us through light fog. I didn't care who it was or who it wasn't; I only cared that it was coming toward us.

It was the *Aikane*, at last, in the end of our strange game of hide-and-seek. I was speechless for a moment, then suddenly the world brightened. My days of facing the unknown alone were over, done, in an instant. We were safe. "Thank you, Lord." Those were the first words I spoke aloud.

And then I rattled off everything to my friends, a disjointed jumble, I'm sure. What a beautiful sight she was, the *Aikane*, a Newporter 40. She held four of my friends on board plus a reporter for Copley News Service. I went on and on and on—about what, I don't recall. I just yammered on until I realized I wasn't too presentable. I had one more job to do.

"Excuse me, please. I'll be back in a minute. Don't go anywhere."

I snuck below for the swiftest bath I'd ever had. I changed into clean white jeans and a sweater, a chiffon scarf, and a gold broach. Twelve minutes from vagabond to debutante, if a little nicked on the edges. When my friend asked whether she could get me anything, I finally asked for it.

"Yes! A cheese sandwich, a glass of milk, and an apple."

We sailed together in a light breeze the entire day, easing our way down the coast. Our best wind came from a press helicopter overhead. Ships blasted their welcome, and an airplane flew above in salute. Reporters from across the country and overseas were calling to *Aikane* for interviews during our slow progress south. *Aikane*'s radiotelephone was overheating. The marine operator had freed one line just for all the calls waiting. It didn't let up. "How does she look?" "What is she wearing?" "Is the boat OK?" Of course, I could only hear one side of the conversations on my shortwave—more frustration. Once again, I couldn't talk back.

When we finally neared Marina Del Rey, more friends sailed out to see us. *Aikane* was like a mother hen, keeping vigil over her chick. At night the only way she could keep track of *Sea Sharp II* was by the dim light of kerosene lamps through my cabin windows. If the wind blew them out—as occasionally happened—they'd shine a spotlight on me or blast their horn to wake me. The *Aikane* became my eyes and ears down the coast.

I slept, sometimes to my detriment. We nearly hit a tugboat towing a barge of rock as it approached perpendicular to our course. My friends on the *Aikane* watched with trepidation as the tug drew nearer. Should they wake me? But lo and behold, *Sea Sharp II* knew what she was doing. At the last minute, she abandoned her course and let the tug go by with no guidance from me.

By the time we reached the outskirts of San Diego, I was well fed. My friend, Ami, had prepared a feast for me. She made everything I was homesick for: a mound of potato salad with carrot sticks and strips of cheese, fried chicken, and sliced ham. She sealed the plate with plastic wrap, slid it into a Ziploc bag, and slipped that inside a plastic laundry bag—ready for home delivery. The package was trailed off the stern of *Aikane* until it came alongside *Sea Sharp II* and I could haul it in.

July 23. 5:15 a.m. I stopped counting. That was the end of our journey. We were inside the San Diego Harbor around Point Loma. It had been seventy-four days, seventeen hours, and fifteen minutes since the last line had been cast off at Yokohama. We were home. I had nothing more to do but put on my pink suit and polish my fingernails.

Remember the Japanese grandmother's gift to me, a one-eyed stuffed head? I added the second eye. At 9:00 a.m. sharp, a harbor fireboat led a procession, and the press boats surrounded me en masse, just as they had on departure day. Whistles tootled, horns honked, people shouted.

Of course Clair was one of those in the fleet, sailing his Mariner 31. He told me later that many days before anyone knew I was safe and coming into the home stretch, he hated to answer his phone. Reporters were haunting him. All he could tell them was, "I know she's all right; she'll make it. . . . She'll be here, she'll be here."

The Yokohama sister-city delegation had come over for the bicentennial ceremonies and had stayed an extra three days, just hoping I would arrive so they could be in my welcoming committee. They were there in spirit when it finally happened.

As we approached the customs dock at Shelter Island, I furled the genny and took down the main for the last time. I had to find my dock lines. The crowd cheered. The harbor officials standing guard at the dock were the first to touch the boat, the first fingers *Sea Sharp II* had felt, other than mine, in seventy-four days. I was a foreign vessel, after all, and I had to clear customs.

Then the press descended upon us. Clair and Mayor Frank Curran led the group down the gangway.

"What's going to be next for you, Sharon?" a reporter asked.

"It's a big world," I said.

This time, I needed no assistance off the boat when it was time to go up the gangway to American soil. The letters and plaques from Japan were delivered as promised. To my astonishment, when I gave Mayor Curran his parchment paper letter from "The Lord Mayor of the Great City of Yokohama" encased in a brocade cardboard folder tied with a silk ribbon, it was the wrong one. Someone in Yokohama had made an ironic faux pas. I was inadvertently delivering the letter of friendship from the square-rigger that had saluted me seventy-two days before. They had been given the one meant for me, and delivered it long before my arrival. It took them a mere twelve days for their crossing.

There were speeches and awards and official handshakes. I was presented with a key to the city. I had already accumulated five others, but that one was special. The San Diego Fire-Rescue Department had used an early California mission gate key as a matrix. Old, bronze fire-hose nozzles were melted down to cast forty of those eight-inch, heavy keys, to which were added the city seal.

My greeting ended with the ringing of the two-and-a-half-ton Yokohama Friendship Bell. It is housed in a specially built Japanese structure on Shelter Island, where it is rung on auspicious occasions.

To this day, I can hear that massive bell's resounding peal of friendship back across the ocean, saying thank you from a grateful American to all the Japanese who had done so much for her.

PART FOUR

In the Wake of Fame

FIFTEEN

Sailing On

I was able to wean myself away from *Sea Sharp II* gradually, for Clair had agreed I could keep her four months. A blessing to me. I hosted a "thank you" dock party for *Sea Sharp II* and fifty people one Sunday afternoon. Everyone who had helped me or who had been involved in my success was invited—Clair, Hugh, Dr. Gold, my wind-vane engineer, my sailmaker, numerous reporters, columnists, faithful believers, and many friends. Guess what: large pink orchids floated in pink champagne punch.

Clair and I put *Sea Sharp II* in the Long Beach boat show, the largest in Southern California. He had a structure built that included a stairway leading up to a deck-level platform, which ran the length of the boat, and a stairway down. The long lines of visitors did not stop for three days. I couldn't even leave for lunch or take a break. Mostly the visitors just asked questions, but a few wanted to go below.

Finally, the day came. It had to come. Clair took *Sea Sharp II* from Marina del Rey, but I wasn't around to see her sail away. I just couldn't do it.

She was gone, and that was it. I went back to being an every-day woman. People tend to think the famous live in a universe of their own, but that is not always the case. At least, it was not the case for me. My life as a celebrated sailor slowly changed after that trip from Yokohama. I had speaking engagements, a National Public Radio interview, a few spots on *The Today Show*, *What's My Line*, *I've Got a Secret*, *The Art Linkletter Show*, and Steve Allen's program. My favorite guest appearance was being interviewed by David Frost. The governor of Michigan even sent me four tickets to the 1970 Rose Bowl on the fifty-yard line. The only problem was the maize and blue pompon I was given to cheer for Michigan; of course, I was rooting for the University of Southern California.

Soon enough the winds calmed, and my little puff of fame luffed like a sail without air.

I lived a private fairy tale for a while. I met my soul mate, master mariner Albert Krystal. He figured if I could sail alone, together we'd be doubly good. We had big dreams. We moved to Perth, Australia, where we were having a boat built, on which we planned to sail the world—to cross the Indian Ocean, see the Seychelles, spend some time on the African coast, and return home via the Panama Canal. We contracted for the boat, but it all went badly. After four months in the boatyard, I could tell what was being built would never be what we had contracted for. We spent the next eight months in court getting our money back.

That killed the fantasy. My captain returned to sea, and I went back to the nine-to-five world as property manager for a real estate company in Santa Monica, California. Albert and I had the best of both worlds. My love would be at sea two to four months, then home for the same. On land, we enjoyed the mountains.

But those times ran short. Eight years was all we had before Albert died of emphysema.

Just as I sailed before the time of women sailors, making single-handed voyages, I caught the coffee craze before its time. I opened a coffee store in a mall in Irvine, California, when almost no one outside of Seattle had heard of Starbucks and long before Frappuccinos and pumpkin-spice lattes had become de rigueur. I held out for two years but eventually sold the business and lost a bundle.

I had just enough to open a mobile hotdog stand on the bike path that follows the beach from Malibu to Redondo. I met many interesting people, world travelers who asked lots of questions, and I would have kept that job, but the third robbery drove me out. I moved my business to the California State University campus at Hayward, where I was known as Grandma the Hotdog Lady. Those students were my kids; some of us still keep in touch.

But age crept up on me, and the long hours and heavy labor conspired against my body. I returned to my beloved Oregon, taking on another property-management job until my sixty-fifth birthday. I retired, bought a mobile home, and surrounded myself with mementos of my former life.

And that's where you'll find me today, in Beaverton, Oregon. My home is the one with a lighthouse mural painted on the front; and in the yard are a miniwharf, seagulls, a propeller, several glass fishnet floats, and a message in a bottle. I garden and hike; I aerobicize and fish. I still give public presentations across the state. I bring my little blue duffel bag with that wild boar's tusk and the New Zealand tiki, and I share my stories from Asia and the South Pacific. I talk to civic groups, schools, nursing homes, churches, and private clubs—anyone who will have me.

Every year during the second week of September, I return to Prineville for a three-day campout on beautiful Ochoco Lake with the class of 1948. I have journeyed far; but in my heart, I've never really left the country I love so dearly. My classmates and I spend our time eating and swapping life stories.

I've been in touch with my children and grandchildren. It's always been tough with Sandy and Dennis. I've never had the right words to describe what happened or to talk with other people about them. I always felt wrong saying I was their mother. A woman doesn't have to give birth to be a mother, and giving birth doesn't always make her one. Yet when people would ask me whether I had children, I hated to deny them. It isn't as bad now; circumstances and lifestyles have changed. But back in my day, you were an awful person if you left your children. You really were the devil.

Yet Sandy and Dennis managed to grow up and succeed without me. My grandchildren, too. Ted, a fireman-paramedic in Eugene, Oregon, served a year in Iraq in the National Guard. I am so proud of him, and thank the Lord he came home unscathed. And my granddaughter, Cyndy, earned her college degree in journalism from the University of Arizona; she's a newspaper reporter in Flagstaff, Arizona. I hear from them from time to time, as well as receive an occasional visit.

One of my public programs paid off in a unique way in 2005. I was to make a presentation to a group at the University of Oregon, Bend campus. My two half-brothers, Walt and Fred, had read about the scheduled event in the newspaper, and they came to hear me. I knew they existed but had heard nothing of them for fifty-seven years. They are both retired. Walt lives in the Bend area, and Fred lives just six miles from me. Imagine! All that time. They have added to my life. We are getting acquainted.

And life sails along.

I'm just me in my mobile home with a few plaques on the wall, surrounded by mementos and a porthole for a window. I have a world of memories to keep me afloat. Before I learned to sail, it had always felt to me as though each day was the same as the one before. I had always felt as though maybe life were just about to begin.

And then, somewhere out on that wide blue ocean, I realized I was living.

Glossary

aft   toward the stern

afterguy   a line used to control movement and stability of a spinnaker pole or boom

azimuth   horizontal direction measured around the horizon, expressed in degrees

backstay   cable running from the masthead to the stern to secure the mast fore and aft

batten   a thin strip of wood or other flexible material fitted to the edge of a sail (in a batten pocket) to give the sail shape and to keep it from curling and cupping the wind

beam   the greatest width of a boat

bilge   the lowest depth of a boat

bitt   a deck post used for securing lines

block   a pulley used for lines

boom   a spar used to secure the foot of a sail

boom crutch   a U-shaped holder for the boom when the sail is down

boom vang   a system used to hold down the boom, especially when sailing downwind, to hold the shape of a sail

boatswain's chair   a seat used to hoist a person aloft to maintain rigging (also called a bosun's chair)

bow   front of the boat

bowline   a type of knot that forms a temporary loop in a line

bow line   a docking line leading from the bow

bowsprit   a short spar extending forward from the bow

cat's paw   very light air rippling the water surface

cleat   a fitting to which a line may be secured

clew   the lower aft corner of a triangular sail to which the sheet is attached

close-hauled   sailing as close to the wind as possible

clinker   built with overlapping planks or boards

clove hitch   a knot used to temporarily fasten a line to a spar

coaming   a vertical framework around the cockpit

cockpit   an open area from which the boat is handled

crow's nest   a structure in the upper mainmast of a ship used as a lookout

dead reckoning   estimating the position of a boat by compass, log, and calculation of time, wind, and current

declination   the angular distance to a point on a celestial object

doldrums   an area of no wind

ease   to slacken the trim of a sail

figure eight   a knot in the form of a figure eight, placed at the end of a line to prevent it from passing through a block

foreguy   a line used to control the movement of the spinnaker pole

forward   toward the bow of the boat; opposite of aft

furl   to roll and secure a sail on a boom

galley   the kitchen area of a boat

gangway   the side of a ship where people board and disembark

genny   genoa

genoa   a large, triangular overlapping sail (also a genny)

halyard   a line used for raising sails

hatch   a covered opening in the cabin to enter the boat

heading   the direction in which the boat is sailing at any given time

headsail   any sail forward of the foremast

helm   a steering device, usually a tiller or wheel, which controls the rudder

hull   the main body of a boat

jib   a triangular foresail smaller than a genoa

jury-rig   to improvise and temporarily repair

keel   a weight at the deepest point of a boat (usually lead), which gives the boat stability

ketch   a two-masted boat with the mizzen mast shorter than the main and located forward of the rudder post

knot one nautical mile per hour (6,076 feet)

latitude distance in degrees north or south of the equator

lazarette a storage space in the cockpit

leech the aft edge of a triangular sail

leeward the direction away from the wind (pronounced loo-ward)

line takes its name from its function (there is no rope on a boat)

logbook a sailor's concise daily record

longitude distance east or west of the meridian through Greenwich, England

luff to let the sail flap either by heading closer to the wind or by slacking the sheets; also the forward edge of a sail

mainmast tallest mast of a ketch

mainsail the largest sail attached to the mast and boom, aft of the mainmast

miter sail pieces sewn together so they form triangles and come together at the clew

mizzen a smaller sail on the aft mast

mizzen mast the aft shorter mast on a ketch or yawl

mooring an arrangement for securing a boat to a buoy or pier

port the left side of a boat when facing forward

preventer a line secured to the outboard end of a boom to limit movement

pulpit a metal framework on deck, providing a safety railing and serving as an attachment for lifelines

reach the point of sailing with wind abeam

reef to reduce sail

rigging the lines and cables that attach sails and spars to the boat (standing: cables that need no adjustment; running: lines used to adjust the sails)

roach the curved portion of extra material on a sail (the portion outside the perfect triangle)

rudder moveable hinged plate under water, which steers the boat when turned

running   sailing with the wind coming from the stern

running lights   navigation lights required on boats from sunset to sunup

scupper   a drain that allows water to run overboard

self-bailing cockpit   a watertight cockpit with scuppers or other devices to remove water

sheet   a line used to trim a sail

shroud   a cable that supports the mast laterally

sloop   a single-masted boat

sole   cabin or cockpit floor to be walked on

spars   the poles in a boat's rigging (masts, booms, etc.)

spinnaker   a three-cornered, parachute-like sail flown from the mast in front of the other sails, used for sailing downwind

spreaders   spars extending laterally from the mast to give shape and stability to the shrouds

squall   a sudden, violent wind, often with rain

stanchions   upright posts used to support life lines

starboard   the right side of a boat when facing forward

stays   cable from the masthead to the bow (headstay) or stern (backstay), supporting the mast

stern   back (aft end) of a boat

storm trysail   heavy small sail attached to the mast but not to the boom in extreme weather

tack   (n) the course a boat is sailing in relation to the wind; (v) to turn the bow through the wind

taffrail   the rail around the stern

taffrail log   a spinner trailed through the water to measure distance traveled

tiller   a bar or handle used for turning a boat's rudder

topping lift   a line or cable that supports the weight of the boom when raising or lowering the sail

topsides   the sides of the boat between the waterline and the deck

transom   the flat or curved structure of the hull at the stern trim   the set of the sails in reference to the angle of the wind

waterline   a line showing the point to which the boat should sit in the water

whisker pole   a light spar for holding a jib when sailing off the wind

winch   a geared device for increasing advantage when raising or trimming sail

windward   toward the direction from which the wind is blowing

zenith   the highest point; the point of sky directly above the sailor

In the Outdoor Lives series

Kayaking Alone
Nine Hundred Miles from Idaho's Mountains to the Pacific Ocean
by Mike Barenti

Bicycling beyond the Divide
Two Journeys into the West
by Daryl Farmer

Pacific Lady
The First Woman to Sail Solo across the World's Largest Ocean
by Sharon Sites Adams with Karen J. Coates